T0302617

Moon Books Duets

Kitchen Witchcraft
&
Moon Magic

Moon Books Duets
Kitchen Witchcraft
&
Moon Magic

Rachel Patterson

MOON
BOOKS
London, UK
Washington, DC, USA

CollectiveInk

First published by Moon Books, 2024
Moon Books is an imprint of Collective Ink Ltd.,
Unit 11, Shepperton House, 89 Shepperton Road, London, N1 3DF
office@collectiveinkbooks.com
www.collectiveinkbooks.com
www.moon-books.net

For distributor details and how to order please visit the 'Ordering' section on our website.

Text copyright: Rachel Patterson 2024

ISBN: 978 1 80341 559 8
978 1 80341 809 4 (ebook)
Library of Congress Control Number: 2024932632

A CIP catalogue record for this book is available from the British Library.

Design: Lapiz Digital Services

UK: Printed and bound by TJ Books Limited, Padstow, Cornwall
Printed in North America by CPI GPS partners

We operate a distinctive and ethical publishing philosophy in
all areas of our business, from our global network of authors to
production and worldwide distribution.

This edition is a bind up of two books:

Pagan Portals – Kitchen Witchcraft
First published by Moon Books 2013
Text copyright: Rachel Patterson 2012
ISBN: 978-1-78099 843-5 (Paperback)
ISBN: 978-1-78099-842-8 (e-book)

Pagan Portal – Moon Magic
First published by Moon Books, 2014
Text copyright: Rachel Patterson 2013
ISBN: 978-1-78279-281-9 (Paperback)
ISBN: 978-1-78279-282-6 (e-book)

Introduction

In another age, in another lifetime, perhaps in another reality, a figure stands hunched over a bubbling cauldron, muttering under their breath and tossing seemingly random herbs and plant matter into the depths. Bunches of herbs and flowers hang over head, drying in the warm air of the kitchen. Bottles, jars and packages filled with seeds, spices and what look suspiciously like small bones are scattered across the heavily worn but cleanly scrubbed wooden table. But is it another time or another age? This could actually be in the here and now, because this is a frequent occurrence for any practicing kitchen witch, in days gone by but also in modern times. The only difference being today the cauldron might be a casserole dish or a slow cooker.

There is magic in all things, there is energy in all things and a witch knows how to connect. Kitchen Witchcraft works with the plants and herbs in your garden and the spices and ingredients in your kitchen cupboards. Everything is filled to brimming over with magic that you could work with to bring about healing, protection, manifesting and more. A kitchen witch uses whatever is to hand, there are no fancy tools or expensive, exotic ingredients. Spells are cast with a pinch of this and a spoonful of that and directed with a flick of the wooden spoon. Magic is created from little or nothing but sends out a powerful punch of energy.

Pagan Portals - Kitchen Witchcraft introduces you to the magic within yourself, your kitchen cupboards and the basic structure of the Craft. Create a sacred kitchen, make friends with your appliances and cook up some real kitchen magic. The book also delves into the foundation of magic such as working with the elements, candle magic and the sabbats. Kick into your Kitchen Witch self by creating some of the suggested crafts with spiritual washes, sprays and spell workings. Follow that with a trip around the magical garden.

There are many things that define a Witch, one of those is perhaps working with the magic of the Moon. She is a powerful energy, one that is strong enough to control the tides of the ocean no less! Moon Magic is about phases and rhythms; it is about stepping into the ebb and flow of her magical and mystical tide of energy. That energy can be used to work magic of all kinds but also to help us understand and work with our emotions, energy levels, feelings and spirituality. *Pagan Portals - Moon Magic* will show you how to tap into that flow to help you in your everyday mundane and magical life.

Understand the lunar cycle and how it all works, then bring in the different phases, all nine of them. Each one allows you to tap into a different energy to work with to boost your magic and live your life in harmony with the flow of lunar energy. Discover the colour magic of each moon phase, herbs, oils and crystals that correspond with each and how to use them for the best advantage. Use the guided meditations for each moon phase to help you connect and understand the nuances of them. Perform different rituals for each moon phase, cast the circles, call the quarters and work the magic that aligns with them.

Find out about the magic behind eclipses, blue moons and seasonal moons and be inspired to keep a moon diary. Discover the connection between the Triple Goddess and the moon phases and what it means to you. Each month has a special moon name and corresponding energies, what is yours called? If you love trees then embrace the idea of the Celtic Tree calendar and how it works with the full moon energy each month. Let me introduce you to a whole host of moon deities, gods and goddesses from across the globe that all carry the moon energy with them.

Instructions and guidance on how to set up a moon altar and to discover your own moon spirit animal and what they mean to you. Participate in the rite of Drawing Down the Moon and the wonderful experience it can bring to the solitary or group practitioner. Interested in astrology? Then take a look at the astrological moon signs, their meanings and correspondences and how they can help boost your magical workings.

Crescents, circles, fish and frogs, just some of the symbols and signs that are associated with the Moon, what others are there and what do they mean? Bring the moon into your home and your garden, particularly with gardening to give the plants an extra surge of growth and success. Make some moon cord magic, by the knot of one, two, three and more! How does cabbage and lettuce figure in moon magic? They are just two items that are associated with the magic of the moon that can help bring about luck and protection. Along with an array of beautiful moon magic crystals. Have a go at scrying under the powerful light of the full moon or stare into a crystal ball, what will you see? Finish up by getting crafty with moon creations and stepping into the Moon tarot card.

Two books packed full with a whole lot of powerful, wonderful and mystical magic, what are you waiting for?

Rachel Patterson – April 2024

About the Author

I am an English witch who has been walking the Pagan pathway for over thirty years. A working wife and mother who has been lucky enough to have had over 25 books published (so far), some of them becoming best sellers. My passion is to learn, I love to study and have done so from books, online resources, schools and wonderful mentors over the years and still continue to learn each and every day, but I have learnt the most from actually getting outside and doing it.

I like to laugh ... and eat cake...

It is my pleasure to give talks to pagan groups and co-run open rituals and workshops run by the Kitchen Witch Coven. I am also High Priestess of the Kitchen Witch Coven and an Elder at the online Kitchen Witch School of Natural Witchcraft.

A regular columnist with Fate & Fortune magazine, I also contribute articles to several magazines such as Pagan Dawn and Witchcraft & Wicca. You will find my regular ramblings on my own personal blog and YouTube channel.

My craft is a combination of old religion witchcraft, Wicca, hedge witchery, kitchen witchery and folk magic. My heart is that of an English Kitchen Witch.

It was my honour to be added to the Watkins 'Spiritual 100 List' for 2023.

www.rachelpatterson.co.uk
facebook.com/rachelpattersonbooks
www.kitchenwitchhearth.net
facebook.com/kitchenwitchuk
Email: HQ@kitchenwitchhearth.net

www.youtube.com/user/Kitchenwitchuk
www.instagram.com/racheltansypatterson

MOON BOOKS

Kitchen Witchcraft Series
Spells & Charms
Garden Magic
Crystal Magic
The Element of Earth
The Element of Fire
The Element of Water

Pagan Portals
Kitchen Witchcraft
Hoodoo Folk Magic
Moon Magic
Meditation
The Cailleach
Animal Magic
Sun Magic
Triple Goddess
Gods & Goddesses of England
Dragon Magic
Sulis

Other Moon Books
The Art of Ritual
Beneath the Moon
Witchcraft ... into the Wilds
Grimoire of a Kitchen Witch
A Kitchen Witch's World of Magical Foods
A Kitchen Witch's World of Magical Plants & Herbs
Arc of the Goddess (co-written with Tracey Roberts)

Moon Books Gods & Goddesses Colouring Book
(Patterson family)
Practically Pagan: An Alternative Guide to Cooking

Llewellyn
Curative Magic
A Witch for All Seasons: Spells, Rituals, Festivals, and Magic
Practical Candle Magic: Witchcraft with Wick & Wax

DECKS
Solarus
Flower Magic Oracle Deck
Animal Dreaming Publishing
Magical Herbs Oracle Deck part of the Kitchen Witch series

MOON BOOKS PUBLISHING
MoonCon (Host)
The Pagan Portal Podcast (Host)

KITCHEN
WITCHCRAFT

CRAFTS OF A KITCHEN WITCH

PAGAN PORTALS

RACHEL PATTERSON

What People Are Saying About

Kitchen Witchcraft

I like this ... it's light, friendly and good fun to read. One important facet of traditional Craft is the use of the kitchen and everyday implements to create magical goodies. I like the way the author brings the reader into the kitchen and makes the whole thing inclusive like having a cosy chat over the cauldron. A great addition to the Pagan Portals series.
Mélusine Draco, author of numerous popular books

Rachel Patterson's *Kitchen Witchcraft* is an excellent introduction to witchcraft's system of correspondences, and reminds us that the ingredients of nature's magic surround us whether we live in an Old World witch's cottage or a modern high rise.
Mark Carter, author of *Stalking the Goddess*

A wonderful little book which will get anyone started on Kitchen Witchery. Informative, and easy to follow.
Janet Farrar & **Gavin Bone**, authors *A Witches Bible, Witches Goddess and Inner Mysteries*

I am very proud to write this endorsement for Rachel's book, *Kitchen Witchcraft*. Rachel is very sensible and down to earth, both qualities that are rare nowadays, but which I really admire. Kitchen Witchcraft is becoming increasingly possible as people try and merge spiritual and everyday life. Rachel's book contains plenty of great suggestions for kitchen witchery and I particularly like her emphasis on learning to love what you have, yet learning to adapt and grow too, which is an essential part of the Craft. The beauty of this book is the ease with which Rachel blends the magical with the everyday, something I consider to be the true essence of all witchcraft. Her writing is a friendly, personal account that immediately invites us to feel we are there in the kitchen with her. This is particularly helpful for those who work as solitaries. *Kitchen Witchcraft* contains plenty of ideas about the seasons, elements, festivals, gardens, working with candles and crystals and – best of all in my view – recipes for potions and incense etc. These will make even the newest beginner feel very 'witchy' indeed!

Tylluan Penry, author of *Seeking the Green, Magic on the Breath, Magical Properties of Plants, Staying on the Old Track* and *the Essential Guide to Psychic Self Defence*

It's a great little book, it's packed with all kinds of information any Pagan would find very useful from candle magic and cleaning fluids to details of the elements. This is something you need to keep handy in your kitchen for helping you with your spells, your incense and your day-to-day magical life.

Siusaidh Ceanadach, author of *A Ceremony for Every Occasion* & *Let's Talk About Pagan Festivals*

Pagan Portals
Kitchen Witchcraft

Rachel Patterson

MOON
BOOKS
London, UK
Washington, DC, USA

Contents

Introduction

A woman stands hunched over an old wooden table, pestle and mortar in her hands, grinding away at a mixture of ingredients. A large white candle stands on the table beside her, the flame flickering and spluttering. Open in front of her lies a huge leather-bound book, the pages well-worn and filled with beautifully written spells. Sounds like a scene from medieval times? Actually, it could be now; it could be me (or you) in a town house kitchen, or an apartment in the city.

This is a witch at work, same scene, same utensils, and same ingredients now as centuries ago.

A witch works with nature, in tune with the earth, working and living along with the ebb and flow of the seasons. Spring is for cleaning, clearing out clutter, sweeping out the cobwebs and setting new goals. Summer is a time for celebrating the Sun God, for basking in his glow, working on projects, gardening and creating. Autumn is a time to be thankful for the harvest, to give thanks for all that we have and to start storing away for the winter. Winter itself is for reflection, a time to pull up a chair by the fire and think back over what you have achieved. All of these things can be done physically, mentally and spiritually with each turn of the Wheel of the Year.

As a witch you can have all the right equipment – wands, athames, pentagrams etc, but you will find a Kitchen Witch tends to prefer to use what is to hand. A finger serves purpose as a wand, a feather for the element of Air, a pebble for the element of earth... you get the drift.

A Kitchen Witch will create... recipes, crafts, lotions and potions. When a friend is poorly a Kitchen Witch will work a spell to aid, but will also make some homemade soup, putting healing energy into making it, adding healing energy with each vegetable and herb that is added.

To connect with the divine a witch will step outside, take a cup of coffee and sit in the garden, to be outside with nature... that is where the connection is. Feel the wind in your hair, the sun on your face, feel the grass beneath your feet, the free and wild feeling of being at one with nature, Mother Earth and her bounty.

A Kitchen Witch will also get that connection in the kitchen, working with herbs, spices, plants and produce. Everything a Kitchen Witch makes is made with love, affection and a little bit of magic.

Here I have shared with you just some of the ways of the witch and the craft, hoping that together we can seek out the Kitchen Witch within.

Kitchen Cupboards and Tools

This is not all that is in my cupboards, but it is a basic list of everyday items to start with.

Salt
Chilli powder
Cinnamon
Paprika
Cloves
Nutmeg
Parsley
Sage
Thyme
Rosemary
Marjoram
Washed, dried and crushed egg shells
Lavender buds
Rose petals

Creating a Sacred Kitchen

So, you might see the kitchen as a wonderful creative space, you might loathe it completely and only ever use the microwave. But it is still a kitchen; it is still a space that you have to make food in. So how about making it a magical space?

In my ideal world I would have a huge farmhouse kitchen with a large wooden kitchen table in the centre for everyone to sit round, the table bleached from being scrubbed over so many years, herbs hanging overhead drying and a huge oven range to cook on... yeah right... I live in a terraced house in the city! OK so it's a nice 1920's terraced house with real fireplaces, but the kitchen is never going to fit a farmhouse table. So, you make the most of what you have.

So, let's imagine that stepping into your kitchen, whether you will only be in there for the six minutes it takes for the microwave to ping or whether you will be in there for a couple of hours baking your own cakes... that it makes you feel magical, that it makes you feel as if you have stepped into a place of power. Well, we can create that.

It doesn't have to take lots of time or money, you don't have to take on board all the ideas given, but it will give you some suggestions.

Make It Yours

Go take a look in your kitchen, yep go on... I will wait...

What do you see? Do you love the decoration? Do you love the colour? Does it look like something from a country kitchen or does it look like something from the local science lab? You need to think of your kitchen as yours, it ought to reflect you and your connection to the divine. Yes, I know we need it to be practical too, but you can 'make it yours'.

Put a pretty rug on the floor (one that can be chucked in the washing machine).

Paint spirals, Goddess symbols, flowers, leaves – whatever takes your fancy – on the cupboard doors or use stencils.

Check out the stores at Samhain, they usually stock lots of interesting bits and pieces that can be used to decorate a witch's kitchen.

Hang up pictures or items from nature on the walls. Go mad, go wild, go funky (my own kitchen has lots of witches on broomsticks hanging from the ceiling, witch balls too, lots of witch figures on shelves and a besom hanging on one wall, although you don't have to be quite that mad).

Make Like Snow White…
Yep, I mean cleaning; yes, I know it's boring. And I don't expect us all to spend hours every day making it clinical, but if the kitchen smells yucky because it's dirty and if you can't actually see the work surfaces because of clutter you aren't going to feel calm and connected in there.

But you can make the cleaning magical and spiritual. Sing as you clean, something pagan that brings the Goddess into the kitchen as you sweep and mop. If you don't know any particular songs just make something up – singing will help the work get done faster too.

I also think that being bare foot helps to connect when you are at home too, not just in the kitchen but all over the house.

Wear a specific apron, I have one that has witchcraft symbols all over it; you could make your own. Keep it as your magical apron, the one that when you put it on turns you into Super Kitchen Witch.

What about cleaning products? Now there are some very good eco-friendly cleaning products on the market, but we haven't all got the endless budget to pay for them, so if you haven't, how about having a go at making your own?

Make a compost bin, use all your fruit and vegetable scraps, and shredded paper, to make your own compost.

Recycle. I am lucky enough to have a recycle collection scheme; they collect paper, plastic and card once a fortnight.

Ju ju your floor wash – make a good strong cup of herbal tea, strain it and add the liquid to your floor wash, it not only makes it smell nice, but if you use herbs that have cleansing and purifying properties you add magic to your wash too. You can even use herbal tea bags.

Once you have done with the actual physical cleaning give the kitchen a smudge with some sage, lavender or rosemary or even an incense stick will do. Waft the smoke into every corner, even into the cupboards.

Once you have finished, stop and look around again, this is your place of being, it is a sacred place now, one that is ready to make magic in. Send out your energy into your kitchen... own it.

Make Friends with the Appliances

Ok so I am not suggesting you give the cooker a name and hold regular conversations with it – unless you want to... But there are usually a lot of electrical appliances in your kitchen and they all rely on energy to work. Being afraid of using those appliances can send out negative vibes and they might be unhappy to cooperate when we need them too. Consider your appliances your allies; they are your household pixies.

A Kitchen Altar

I think having an altar in your kitchen gives it a focal point; it doesn't have to be big. I have a small green man shelf and on top of that I have a tiny vase (it is actually a small candle holder) that I put a fresh flower in regularly, and it has representations of the elements – a shell, a feather, a red crystal and a pebble. The top of the shelf surface is no bigger than the palm of my hand. You could just have a Goddess statue on a shelf or even just a Goddess picture hung on the wall. Your kitchen altar is where you honour deity as a Kitchen Goddess. You might like to actually choose a particular Goddess to have as your kitchen deity, one that is connected to home and hearth, or you might just want to keep it general – it is your kitchen, your choice. You might even prefer to have a kitchen faerie or a kitchen dragon instead.

You could use candles, these are representations of the element of Fire, which is very prominent in a kitchen, and it also represents the home and hearth. It could even just be a small tea light. You could light the candle when you begin the food preparation, use it as your way to honour deity, light it and ask them to bless the food you are about to prepare.

Leave an offering on your kitchen altar for each meal you prepare (just remember to leave something not too sticky, and remove it the following day).

Have fun with your altar design, use natural objects, and decorate it for the seasons with an acorn, leaves or flowers. If you have the space, you could even go to town on it and decorate it with kitchen items – cutlery, tiny pots or pans from dolls house furniture.

Whatever you end up creating for your altar and however big or small it is, use it as a focal point in your kitchen. Just take a moment before you start to prepare a meal by standing in front of the altar and asking for a blessing.

Cooking Up Some Magic

OK, so you don your 'Kitchen Witch' apron, your kitchen is all tidy, and your altar is all pretty. Then what?

Even the most domesticated goddess won't feel like cooking every single day, so just give yourself a few moments before you start to get yourself in the right frame of mind, stand in front of your altar or your Goddess picture/statue and calm, centre and ground yourself.

If you are making a meal for yourself or to share you don't want to be doing it whilst sending out negative energies. Part of the cooking process allows you to 'add' magic to the meal, whether it is in the form of herbs, ingredients or just the positive energy you use whilst you cook. Even if the only cooking you do is to open the packet and warm it up.

Whilst you are preparing your meal try to think and feel positive, whilst you are stirring the pots try to stir them deosil (clockwise) to bring good energies in. As you add ingredients really take notice of their colour, their shape, their energy, the connection they had with the earth.

And, of course, you can tailor your ingredients for the meal you are making. If you are making a romantic meal for a loved one you could add items that have love as one of their magical properties such as cloves or basil or make a pie from apples – charging the ingredients with your intent. If you are making a dish for the family, you could add cinnamon as this brings the magical properties of a happy home, safety and protection. I have listed here some of the more common herbs and foods with their magical properties, there are more detailed lists on the net, but go with your instincts too.

You know the archetypes, like asparagus and oysters being aphrodisiacs, but there are many other foods that have magical properties such as:

Black pepper – stimulating
Cabbage – luck
Carrots – healing
Cashew – money
Celery – mental powers, lust, psychic powers
Chilli pepper – hex breaking, love
Chocolate – comforting
Coriander – stimulating
Corn/maize – protection, luck

Cucumber – chastity, healing, fertility
Grape – fertility, mental powers, money
Onion – strengthening and purifying
Leek – love, protection, exorcism
Lemon – longevity, purification, love, friendship
Lettuce – chastity, protection, love, sleep
Lime – healing, love, protection
Olive – healing, peace, fertility, protection, lust
Onions – protection, exorcism, healing, money, prophetic dreams, lust
Orange – love, luck, money
Pea – money, love
Peach – love, exorcism, longevity, fertility, wishes
Pear – lust, love
Pecan – money, employment
Pepper, black – protection, exorcism
Pineapple – luck, money, chastity
Pomegranate – luck, wishes, wealth, fertility
Potato – good for rheumatism
Rice – protection, rain, money, fertility
Spinach – mental and physical stimulant
Strawberry – love, luck
Sugar – love, lust
Tea (black) – riches, courage, strength
Tomato – prosperity, protection, love
Walnut – health, mental powers, infertility, wishes
Wheat – fertility, money

And herbs:

Allspice – money, luck, healing
Anise – protection, purification, youth
Balm, lemon – love, success, healing
Basil – love, wealth, protection

Bay – protection, psychic powers, healing, purification, strength

Cardamom – lust, love

Chamomile – money, sleep, love, protection, calming, sleep

Cinnamon – spirituality, success, healing, power, psychic powers, lust, protection, love

Clove – protection, love, money

Coriander – love, health, healing

Dill – protection, money, lust, love

Fennel – protection, healing, purification

Fenugreek – money

Garlic – protection, healing, lust

Ginger – love, money, success, power

Juniper – protection, love, exorcism, health

Lavender – love, protection, sleep, chastity, purification, happiness, peace

Marjoram – protection, love, happiness, health, money

Mint – money, lust, healing, exorcism, protection

Nettle – exorcism, protection, healing, lust

Nutmeg – luck, money, health, fidelity

Parsley – lust, protection, purification

Rosemary – protection, love, lust, mental powers, exorcism, purification, healing, sleep, youth

Sage – immortality, longevity, wisdom, protection, wishes

Thyme – health, healing, sleep, psychic powers, love, purification, courage

Turmeric – purification

Vanilla – love, lust, mental powers

Cooking with the Wheel of the Year

I think working with the seasons in your kitchen is very important. For a start, fruit and vegetables taste better when they are in season as they have been allowed to grow naturally at the proper time of the year and haven't been forced. Organic vegetables are obviously best if you can use them because again, they taste better and they are seasonal, but I do appreciate that we can't always afford them. We have an organic vegetable box scheme where I live and, although the price is comparable with the organic vegetables in the supermarket, they are still more expensive than non-organic so I have a box delivered every other week. It's like a lovely surprise every fortnight as I don't know what will be in the box. I try to buy locally when I can too; it's not so easy in the city, but do have a look in your locality for farm shops or farmers' markets.

Not only do you get the better tasting produce when you eat seasonally, I think it helps connect you with the turning of the Wheel too. Fresh sweet strawberries in the summer months make you think and feel of warm summer days, pumpkins and squashes make you think of fallen leaves and dark evenings. It all helps to keep you in touch, to keep that connection to the earth and her cycles. It will also help you to keep track of the Sabbats and understand them more fully. You don't have to prepare a grand feast for each one, but have a think at least about what food our ancestors would have eaten when they celebrated.

And, of course, there are breads and cakes that you could make specifically for Sabbats and Esbats, crescent-shape cookies are fantastic for moon celebrations.

If you harvest a lot of herbs that you won't use all at once, if you dry them for magical uses you can also freeze them, make herbal tea blends; make herb jellies, vinegars and oils with them too.

Witchy Workings in the Kitchen

You can work some spells in the kitchen using the items you have and the produce you use, here are some ideas:

- To release pent up emotions – this one has got to be so simple… chop onions. Let the emotions flow as your tears flow from the onions.
- Release of anger – chop, chop like you have never chopped before. But please be careful of your fingers. Tenderising meat is good for this too, but be careful not to beat it too much!
- Releasing old habits – peel those root vegetables, as you take off the old skin release your old habits, as you see the fresh, clean surface underneath visualize a refreshed you.
- To boost your energy – shake it baby. Make a salad dressing in a jar and shake it, dance round the kitchen with it.
- To bring peace and calm – make something that requires looking after and stirring, such as risotto or a custard, feel yourself becoming calmer and more peaceful with each turn of the spoon.
- To ground – well this one should be obvious – grab yourself a potato or a parsnip, something that has grown in the soil. Hold onto it and connect with its earth energies.
- Bringing things together – to gain balance – try blending or whisking, mixing up batter, something that involves bringing different ingredients together to make a whole.

When Inspiration Escapes

Even though I love to cook some days I just don't feel inspired, it is these days that I sometimes cave in and order takeaway and that's OK, we all need a day off and a treat now and then. On other days when inspiration has departed and I don't have the funds for takeaway I get out my cook books and look for inspiration or watch a food channel on TV. Or if you have the time, go out and have a wander around your local farm shop or farmers' market; be inspired by the produce itself.

You might also find that what you feel like cooking will change depending on where your body is in its cycle, where the moon is in her phase or how you are feeling – keep an eye on it and see if you can note any patterns.

It's Not All About Food

What? I hear you cry... surely, it's always about food? Ha! nope. Your witchy kitchen is also a good place to make lotions and potions. You can make lots of lovely body lotions in your kitchen too, along with bath salts, balms and incense. You could also make your own perfume blends, herbal sachets, pressed flowers, smudge sticks and medicine bags.

What Does a Kitchen Witch Use for Magical Tools?

- Cauldron – a casserole dish or Dutch oven. Make sure it is an old one or one you don't mind being spoilt because as you burn things in it, it will remove any non-stick surface.
- Wand – I have made wands myself from sticks and twigs. You can also use your finger or a wooden spoon works very well too.
- Athame – a kitchen knife or even a potato peeler.
- Chalice – a pretty glass or cup – sometimes you can find really nice pieces in the charity shops/thrift stores.
- Candlesticks – I have two very pretty silver candlesticks to hold my Goddess and God candles, I purchased them for a few pence in a charity shop.
- Pentacle – this can be made from all sorts of natural items – sticks and twigs bound together with hemp string look really effective. Or you could draw a pentagram on a round flat pebble from the beach. If you are any good with a needle you could make a cross stitch or embroidered one.

- Offering dish – I have a couple of dishes that I put crystals or herbs in when I am making a request to deity or thanking them. One I made myself, which is very basic, I formed from air drying clay (it was only a few pence from a local craft store) and the other is just a large round flat shell I found on the beach.
- Elements – to represent the elements you can use a pebble or a dish of soil or salt for Earth, a feather or incense for Air, a candle for Fire or I sometimes use a red coloured crystal, and for Water a small dish of water or a shell works perfectly.

Celebrating the Sabbats

We celebrate the Sabbats to mark the turning of the Wheel of the Year to walk the path our ancestors followed in honouring the Earth and the seasons.

Yule

Yule is a time of rebirth, when the sun stops retreating and stands still (which is the meaning of the word solstice) then begins to return.

This is a time to dance, sing and feast. Make a Yule log, hang mistletoe, drink wassail, light candles, decorate your Yule tree and celebrate the blessings of having family and friends.

It is also the time when the Holly King, who represents winter, fights with the Oak King, who represents summer. They battle and the Holly King is defeated, the Oak King stands to reign until the Summer Solstice.

I don't necessarily like the cold, but I do love the festive season, always have done ever since I was a child. My parents made a huge effort at this time of the year and still do and I have followed on in the tradition.

To me Yule is a magical time, it is all about family and friends. It is celebrating what we have and who we have to share it with. The nights are dark, but we have warm homes to stay inside and keep us protected. We have loving family and friends to share our time with, and whilst I am not a big lover of snow from the practical point of view it does look so beautiful when it is first laid, so white and pure and untouched, very magical indeed.

I have two large Yule trees, one in the dining room that is decorated with reds and golds, plus lots of natural decorations as well. Then I have a tree in the lounge too that is all decorated with greens and golds and our bauble collection. Each year that my husband and I have celebrated a Yule together we have purchased a special tree bauble, they are all shapes and sizes and sometimes represent something from that year. And once our children came along, they have had a bauble for each Yule they have celebrate. They get to choose it.

My main altar will be decorated with red and gold and sparkly faerie lights, my working altar will also be red and gold. Lots of candles and lots of glitter. I also have fake flowers – mistletoe, ivy, holly and pine cones – that I use as well.

I also make an extra effort over the winter months to make sure there is plenty of food out in the garden for the birds.

- Foods for Yule – nuts, apples, cider, pork, dried fruit, cookies, mulled wine.
- Colours for this celebration are red, green, white, gold and silver.
- Make incense using cedar, ginger, cinnamon, pine, rosemary, frankincense, myrrh, nutmeg and cloves.
- Decorate with candles, evergreens, holly, mistletoe, lights, Yule log, wreaths and bells.

Imbolc

Imbolc is when the first signs of spring growth are seen. Underneath the Earth new life is stirring.

This festival is sacred to the Goddess Brighid, the Goddess of healing, poetry and fire. She breathes life into the Earth wiping away the darkness of the winter. This festival honours the Goddess in her Maiden form as she waits for the return of the sun. It is a time for new beginnings and renewal.

For me after Yule there is a bit of a dip, a bit of a lull. January for me is a quiet, non-event kind of a month. The festivities are over, probably in the days of our ancestors' food stores were beginning to run low, the weather is always cold, snowy or wet and no one has any money. But it is also the start of the new calendar year, full of possibilities and promises. A time to stay inside and take stock and plan all the wonderful things to do for the coming year. And as Imbolc comes upon us hopefully there are a few odd signs the spring is on its way. Imbolc is all about the returning light, the days are ever so slowly getting longer, the dark nights getting ever so slowly shorter.

My altar will be decorated a white cloth, I will have lots of white, pale green and pale-yellow candles and will put some greenery from the garden in a vase. I have a couple of variegated evergreen shrubs in the garden so the white and green go very well with Imbolc.

- Foods for Imbolc – spicy dishes, dairy, seeds, herbal teas, garlic and onions.
- Colours for this celebration are pale blue, pale pink, white, yellow and pale green.
- Make incense using basil, bay, chamomile, cinnamon, sage, frankincense, myrrh, sandalwood, vanilla and violet.
- Decorate with candles, lights, besoms, flowers, Brighid's crosses, horseshoes, seeds and seasonal flowers.

Ostara

Ostara is a festival of fertility of the land and marks the time when day and night are equal in length. It is a time for new beginnings, fertility, wishes, rebirth, renewal, bringing your desires into your life.

The God and the Goddess are courting at this time, so it is a good time to focus on the balance between male and female energies within ourselves.

And it's all about the chocolate. Spring is bursting out all over as they say. Ostara is fresh, it is the earth waking up and starting to show the signs of life, plants and animals beginning the journey towards the summer months. It is fertility in an eggshell, literally. The egg symbolises new life, new hope and the promise of expectation. It is a time to start new projects, to begin a new phase of your life.

My altar will be decorated with white or yellow cloth, and then covered with tiny fluffy chicks and lambs (not real ones obviously…) I also have some beautiful tiny painted china eggs that I hang on my main altar. Hopefully the camellia will be flowering in my garden too and I like to float some of the flowers from that in a small dish of water on the altar too.

- Foods for Ostara – eggs, edible flowers, fish, sweet breads, chocolate, honey cake, dairy, nuts and seasonal fruit.
- Colours for this celebration are pale green, bright green, pale blue, pale yellow, pale pink and white.
- Make incense with violet, ginger, broom, sage, lavender, rose and strawberry.
- Decorate with coloured eggs, butterflies, spring flowers, lambs, rabbits, hares and chicks.

Beltane

Beltane is a time when we celebrate fertility, with the sacred marriage of the God and Goddess. This is all about celebrating life! It is the Earth awakening from her sleep and putting forth new growth. Flowers and plants are all starting to bloom and summer is not too far away. Traditionally it is time for the Bel fire, lit from the nine sacred woods – birch, oak, rowan, willow, hawthorn, hazel, apple, grapevine and fir. The fire is healing and purifying and symbolises the burning away of winter and the fruitfulness of summer.

Beltane is all about sex basically. It is the union of the God and the Goddess. In ancient pagan times it was the festival where men and women got together literally to celebrate.

It is May Day; it is the maypole which is basically ahem... male... and danced around by nubile young virgins hoping for that special man to whisk them away. The maypole is quite often red and white striped – the red symbolising the female the white symbolising the male.

My altar will be decorated with a red cloth with red and white candles. By this time there will hopefully be some early roses in the garden to put in a vase.

This is the time of the year when plans you put into action should be starting to happen, if they aren't, it is time to sort them out and set them in the right direction.

It is also usually the time when my chimenea gets its first use of the year, I do love to burn my spells! Beltane is also a fire festival, so I like to work with the element of Fire to complement the Sabbat.

- Foods for Beltane – dairy, sweets, custards, ice cream, honey, salads, fruit punch, oat cakes and fruits.
- Colours for this celebration are red and white to represent the God and the Goddess, dark green, blue, pastel colours and yellow.
- Make incense with frankincense, lilac, rose, vanilla, honeysuckle, lavender, patchouli, meadowsweet and sandalwood.
- Decorate with maypoles, baskets of flowers, eggs, chalices and candles to represent fire.

Litha

Litha is the peak of the seasonal cycle, when the hours of daylight are longest. It is a time to soak up the sun, to celebrate the end of the waxing year and to welcome in the waning year. It is also a fertility festival. This is also one of the Sabbats where the veil between our world and that of the Faerie is thin, so we also welcome them.

Summer should be warm hazy days, fields of long grass, butterflies flittering in and out, bees buzzing, but in the UK, we can't always guarantee that.

However, Litha is when the sun is at its highest, the longest day of sunlight and the shortest night. Then it is the slippery slope heading towards the darker half of the year. The Holly King and the Oak King fight again at this point, the Holly King winning this time to rule the dark half of the year.

It seems quite a bitter sweet celebration really, we celebrate the Sun King in all his glory, we thank him for sending the light and the warm to grow the crops and the food, but then we are also saying farewell to him too.

Not long after Litha are the school holidays so I spend a lot more time outside than I do in the school term, trying to prise my children from the computer to play outside. I also spend a lot of time in the garden during the spring and summer months. I like to go out first thing in the morning and say hello to the world and put bread out for the birds, I then go out again in the evenings to water all the plants and potter about dead heading withered flowers and tidying up. I also like to eat my lunch in the garden if I can too; it is my quiet time, the time to connect with nature and be at one. My altar will be decorated with a yellow and gold cloth, yellow candles and fresh flowers from the garden.

- Foods for Litha are honey, vegetables and fruit, bread, ale and mead.
- Colours for this celebration are white, red, yellow, green and blue.

- Make incense with chamomile, copal, fennel, lavender, lemon, oak, pine, sandalwood, thyme and ylang ylang.
- Decorate with symbols of the sun, sunflowers, oak leaves, fresh flowers, fruit, seashells and images of Faerie.

Lughnasadgh

Lughnasadgh is the first harvest; we celebrate abundance and prosperity. The sun is losing its power; although not gone yet, he wanes. A time of reaping what we have sown, not only from the harvest point of view, but also personally.

My working altar will be decorated with yellow and gold material, it will have gold and yellow candles and a vase with fresh flowers in. I will make a salt dough wreath with flowers and leaves on it that I hang above my altar. Living in the centre of the city it is difficult to connect with the essence of the harvest, but on our trips out we pass fields full of grain. In my own small garden, I harvest herbs regularly and collect seed heads from those plants that flower early. The herbs I dry on trays in the conservatory. I also get together with family, where we sit and drink, eat and talk, I would imagine after the harvest our ancestors would have sat back even if only for a short while and feasted and made toasts to the harvest. Also called Lammas, this is the Christian word meaning 'loaf mass' when newly baked loaves are placed on the altar.

- Foods for Litha – bread, nuts, crab apples, rice, lamb, wine, ale, cider, herbal tea, grains, berries and vegetables.
- Colours for this celebration are yellow, gold, orange, green, brown.
- Make incense with rose, rosemary, chamomile, sandalwood, heather, clover, basil, mint and woods.
- Decorate with corn, cornucopias, sheaves of grain, vegetables and fruit, corn dollies, bread, a sickle and fresh flowers.

Mabon

Mabon is the last harvest. It is also the Autumn Equinox when day and night are equal. A time to give thanks to the sunlight and prepare for the winter months ahead. Honour your ancestors, finish up projects and make ready for the darker, colder months to follow.

To me Mabon is the beginning of autumn; it is when the weather starts to change. The mornings become crisp and fresh, there is that slight chill in the air. The leaves are starting to tinge their way to autumn colours. The last of the harvest is being brought in and people and animals are starting to make preparations for the coming winter months. You still get warm days though and we make the most of them. I spend time in the garden tidying up and clearing away the end of the summer bedding plants, cutting back the clematis and the roses. It is a time to celebrate the abundance that nature has provided over the warmer months. It is apple time! Apples seem to represent Mabon perfectly. They have spent the summer months growing and are picked in the autumn, some to be eaten straight away, others to be stored to last through the darker winter months. And if you cut an apple through the centre, you see the pentagram, the sign of the witch and for me Mabon heralds the beginning of the Season of the Witch! The darker months when we spend a lot more time indoors, in front of the fire, reading, cooking, eating, spending time with family and cooking up ideas, spells and schemes!

My altar will be decorated with orange, red and yellow cloth, the candles will also be of the same colour. I will put out apples and the last of the flowers from the garden. I will also put some nuts on it too.

- Foods for Mabon – bread, nuts, apples, root vegetables, squashes and pomegranates.

- Colours for this celebration are brown, red, orange, yellow, gold and purple.
- Make incense with frankincense, sandalwood, juniper, pine, oak, honeysuckle, marigold and rose.
- Decorate with gourds, pine cones, vines, seeds and sun symbols.

Samhain

Samhain is when we mark the end of the seasonal year, when we store away for the following year, when the veil between the worlds is thin and we celebrate those who have gone before us. It is a spiritual time and one that works well for divination and scrying.

The witches' new year, probably the most celebrated witches' Sabbat I would think and of course … trick or treating… and my birthday!

I love this time of the year (and not just coz of the presents…) I love autumn; the crisp fresh air, the crunch of the leaves under foot, the evenings drawing in, the promise of warm nights indoors with a good book and a big bowl of casserole.

It is a time of introspection, a time to look back over all that has occurred over the previous months. Looking at the projects that were started, ones that have worked, ones that have failed, examining them all and re-evaluating.

I always decorate the house and we do get a lot of trick or treaters. I move the furniture in my lounge so that I can put a sideboard in the bay window and I decorate it as a Samhain altar – pumpkins, cobwebs, candles, bats – all the Halloween decorations! I always dress up too.

Samhain is a good time to connect with spirit. I usually put up an ancestors' altar with black and white photographs of my grandparents and great grandparents. I like to scry with water and use the crystal ball too. Along with all the decorations in the house my working altar and my main altar will also be decorated. Black altar clothes, lace, orange and black candles – I even have black roses.

I also make Mexican hot chocolate (hot milk, melted chocolate squares, cinnamon, cardamom and cloves).

- Foods for Samhain – apples, gourds, nuts, squashes, pumpkin, cider, beef, pork, poultry, cakes for the dead, spices and garlic.
- Colours for this celebration are orange, black, red, brown, white, gold and silver.
- Make incense with mint, nutmeg, myrrh, copal, clove, basil, frankincense, lilac, yarrow and ylang ylang.
- Decorate with bat symbols, black cat, spider and wolf images, ghosts, goblins, Jack-o'-lanterns, besoms and pumpkins.

The Moon

So why do we celebrate the moon and why is it so important to a witch?

The waxing moon is when the moon is a crescent in the sky and gaining her power, working her way up to becoming a full moon. Energy is building, and it is a good time to go with the flow and build up your own energy too. Touch base with friends, plan meetings and communicate.

- Waxing moon magic/first quarter – good for courage, elemental magic, friends, luck and motivation. Gives vitality, courage and strength. Stimulates the heart.

The new moon is the Maiden aspect of the Goddess; a time of new beginnings, a time of possibility and opportunity. This is a wonderful time to make new beginnings of all types. It is also a good time to start something creative. New projects at work can also be launched. A good time to apply for jobs or go house hunting.

- New moon magic – good for beauty, health, self-improvement; farms and gardens; job hunting; love and romance, networking. It is good for protection and creates a shield for the beginning of the cycle.

The time of the full moon is the Goddess in her full power, the tides of the seas and the energy in our own bodies are at the highest point. She is full, round and plump, she is the Mother aspect of the moon. Energies will be high at this time, so do watch out for any troubles that might raise their heads. It is a good time to work with divination and to reflect on your goals and feelings.

- Full moon magic – good for artistic endeavours, beauty, health, fitness, change and decisions. Children, competition, dreams, families, health and healing, knowledge and legal undertakings. Love and romance, money, motivation, protection, psychism and self-improvement.

The waning moon is when the moon goes from full back to crescent, when she is on the descent heading towards the dark moon. The energy is waning. Follow the rhythm, clear out rubbish, de-clutter and clean the house. Follow your instincts. This is also a good time to get rid of bad habits and negative energies.

- Waning moon magic/last quarter – good for addictions, divorce, health and healing, banishing disease, stress protection. Transformation from negative vibrations to positive. Balances the energy within the body and helps the mind and body flow more easily with life.

The dark moon, two days before the new moon, is the time of the Crone. A time for inner work, for reflection and introspection.

- Dark moon – good for tackling addictions, change, divorce, enemies, justice, obstacles, quarrels, removal, separation, stopping stalkers and theft. Universal love of self and others. Draws love to you and removes sorrows and past hurts. Calming, protective, serene and improving relationships.

The phases of the moon are the same all over the Earth. When it is a full moon in Britain it is also a full moon in Australia, China and the United States. Work with the phases of the moon for your spell workings; it will add power to them. You can always adjust of course, if you wanted to work a healing spell then for a waning moon you would concentrate on banishing the illness, on a waxing moon you would focus on increasing health and well-being.

Observing the moon phases, celebrating them and working with the energies are ways we tune into universe, to work with deity and learn to go with the ebb and flow of energies.

The Elements

So, what do we do with them?

Well, in ritual we call upon the four quarters/elements to join us, aid us and protect us. We bring all the four elements together with spirit to complete the circle. We can also call upon their powers when working spells.

Each and every person will have characteristics from each element within them and their personality. Using the four elements you can help balance yourself.

Working with the Elements

Suggestions for working with the elements; if you can't get outside to work with the elements direct, work with the crystals suggested in the chart below – meditate using them and visualize the element itself, draw a picture, or print one from the internet or look in a book at an image of the elemental for each element and meditate; research the animals that are associated with each element. Pick one or two of the scents that are associated with each element and wear them.

For each activity you do, make a mental note of how it feels, how you think you are connecting with that element, what smells there are, what you sense.

>   **Earth:** Do gardening, cook, walk in the forest, walk across fields, do mountain climbing, visit a garden or a garden centre, work with herbs, recycle, pick up litter, plunge your hands into a pot of fresh earth.
>
>   **Air:** Go outside when it is windy and let the air blow through you, sit on top of a hill or mountain, check the air quality in your area, and open a window. Fly a kite, watch the birds, lie on your back and watch the clouds, burn incense.

Fire: Have a bonfire or a BBQ, meditate watching a candle flame, sit and watch an open fire, watch fireworks.

Water: Go swimming, splash in puddles, walk in the rain, visit a pond or the seashore, wash the car, water the plants, take a bath or a shower and connect with the essence of water.

Earth

What comes to mind when you think about the element Earth? The first thing I think of is soil, the brown stuff I plant things into in my garden. The soil contains and stores all the minerals and moisture plants need to live. Earth is everything we are, and everything we have comes from this element. We come from it, and at the end of our lives we return to it.

No wonder the Earth element is associated with abundance and prosperity. Earth is where things grow and have their foundation. This is where the association with abundance and prosperity comes from.

Earth is also rock and stones, it makes up the foundation of our planet. It stabilises and grounds us. One of my favourite grounding exercises is to visualize myself as a tree. My roots growing down into the soft, brown soil. Wriggling my roots into it, down to the core of the very planet itself.

Earth is associated with North, with the season of winter and the advancement of old age. Winter, to me at least, is a time of reflecting. The trees and plants and even the animals have all withdrawn into Mother Earth to recuperate, to replenish, ready to venture forth in the spring, renewed and refreshed.

Don't forget to look after this element, the planet, the environment around you. It can even be something small like picking up a piece of litter.

Earth has the colours of the season of winter; those of the dark nights, brown soil, dark grassy landscape and the white of frost and snow. It is also the time of the Cailleach; she is the Goddess of Winter.

To represent this element, you could use a small dish of soil, an earthenware dish, a stone, a pebble, a crystal or even a piece of wood.

Direction: North
Nature: Fertile, nurturing, stabilising, grounding
Elemental: Gnome
Colours: Green, brown, black, grey, white
Places: Caves, forests, groves, valleys, fields, farms, gardens, parks, kitchens, basements, mines, holes
Magic: Money, prosperity, fertility, stability, grounding, employment, material matters
Herbs/plants: Patchouli, vertivert, moss, nuts, roots, barley, cotton, cypress, fern, honeysuckle, horehound, knotweed, mugwort, oats, potato, primrose, rhubarb, rye, sorrel, tulip, turnip, wheat
Stones: Emerald, peridot, agate, apache tear, aventurine, orange calcite, carnelian, diamond, fluorite, jade, jasper, jet, malachite, petrified wood, ruby, sugilite, tiger eye, black or green tourmaline, unakite
Metals: Iron, lead
Animals: Dog, horse, earthworm, gopher, ant, cow, burrowing animals, wolf, bear
Season: Winter
Time: Night
Tool: Pentacle
Signs: Taurus, Virgo, Capricorn
Sense: Touch
Symbols: Salt, clay, soil, rocks, wheat, acorns
Magic type: Gardening, magnet, image, stone, tree, knot, Binding

Air

What do you think of when you think of the element of Air? The image of a bright blue sky with wispy white clouds comes to my mind. The sky is limit less; you can't see an end to it.

Air is all about intellect, truth and knowledge. Air means truth, truth in who you really are and the freedom that comes with that realisation.

Think about the qualities of the wind too, when it whips up the leaves and sends them dancing around. When a wisp of breeze catches your hair. There is nothing quite like the feeling of standing on top of a windy hill with your arms outstretched just letting the wind wrap around you. Don't forget that Air also has its destructive side, think of hurricanes and tornadoes.

Air represents East, the season of spring and youth. It is the place of hope and new beginnings. We get up, we start each new day fresh with new opportunities to learn and grow. We go out into the world to go about our business.

Spring has the same feeling – fresh, new energy. We have hibernated over winter, dreaming and planning. Now it is time to put those plans into action.

Youth is an exciting and even slightly scary time. We set out on our own, starting to explore the big world for ourselves. New experiences, new people, new ventures. This is the time when we start to discover who we are.

Air is associated with thoughts. We need Air to breath, and therefore to live. The Air we breathe in allows us to think clearly, to clear our minds.

Air has the colours of spring: yellow of the rising sun, the light blue of the sky and white of the clouds. Even pale green and pink of new foliage and blossom of Bride, the Goddess of Spring.

To represent the element of Air you might like to use feathers, incense or spring flowers.

Direction: East
Nature: Flying, moving, intelligence
Elemental: Sylph
Colours: Yellow, pale blue, pink, light green
Places: Mountain tops, plains, cloudy skies, high towers, airports, schools, libraries, offices, travel agents, psychiatrist therapy rooms
Magic: Travel, instruction, study, freedom, knowledge, recovering lost items, creativity, visions, psychic power
Herbs/plants: Any flowers, agaric, agrimony, anise, benzoin, bergamot, bittersweet, borage, bracken, brazil nut, broom, caraway, chicory, dock, endive, fenugreek, hazel, hops, lemongrass, mace, maple, marjoram, meadowsweet, mint, mistletoe, palm, parsley, pecan, pine, rice, sage, slippery elm
Stones: Pumice, mica, amethyst, azurite, beryl, blue lace agate, carnelian, chrysoprase, citrine, diamond, fluorite, moldivite, opal, pearl, snow quartz, sapphire, sodalite, blue topaz, blue tourmaline, turquoise
Metals: Tin, copper
Animals: Spider, birds, winged insects
Season: Spring
Time: Dawn
Tool: Wand
Signs: Gemini, Libra, Aquarius
Sense: Hearing, smell
Symbols: Feathers, incense, flowers
Magic type: Divination, concentration, visualisation, wind magic

Fire

What do you think of when you think about the element of Fire? I visualize a huge bonfire, glowing red, yellow and orange or a huge pile of crackling logs and sticks. I can hear spitting sparks of flame and feel the heat on my face.

Fire brings warmth, comfort and protection. It is the light in the dark that drives away outside threats. Fire brings people together, as a community. Although most houses now don't have open fires in each room, a lot still have fireplaces. The hearth is the centre of a home.

Fire is passion; it is the burning flame inside that gives us excitement, energy and strength. It is the fire within us that helps us to meet the challenges that life brings to us. Fire also sparks our imagination, lights our desires and fills us with enthusiasm and encouragement.

Fire can also be destructive, but in that destruction comes renewal and rebirth – think of the phoenix rising from the ashes.

The warning that comes with fire is that it does need to be kept in check. A fire that causes rage can get out of hand.

Cast your mind to the blacksmith's forge. The blacksmith takes raw material, heats it in the fire and creates something new from it. A transformation, this we can do with our own selves.

The fire within you is your own personal power. It is the force that gives you confidence, it takes away the fear and challenges you to push yourself that bit further.

Fire represents the South, the season of summer and adulthood. The sun is at its highest point, it is when we put all our energy into projects and help them grow and mature. The projects that were started in the spring are now flourishing. It is a time for energy, activity and passion. A time to laugh, dance, sing and have fun.

Adults have experience; experience of life and who they are. By adulthood you should have found your place in the world. You have responsibilities, control of your life and your expectations. Just remember to enjoy yourself too, find your inner passion and run with it.

Fire is the colour of summer: the reds of a beautiful sunset, the yellow of the sun and even the green and bright colours of summer flowers and plants. I think of Belenos the Celtic Sun God.

To represent Fire the most obvious item is a candle, especially a red one. You could also use a red stone/crystal.

Direction: South

Nature: Purifying, destructive, cleansing, energetic, sexual, forceful

Elemental: Salamander

Colour: Red

Places: Desert, hot spring, volcano, oven, fireplace, bedroom, locker room, sauna, sports field

Magic: Protection, courage, sex, energy, strength, authority, banishing, negativity

Herbs/plants: Stinging nettles, thistles, chillies, cacti, coffee, seeds, alder, allspice, anemone, angelica, ash, basil, bay, betony, chrysanthemum, cinnamon, clove, coriander, cumin, curry, dill, dragon's blood, fennel, carnation, carrot, cashew, cedar, fig, frankincense, garlic, ginger, hawthorn, juniper, lime, lovage, mandrake, marigold, mustard, nutmeg, oak, orange, holly, rosemary, pepper, pomegranate, tobacco, walnut, witch hazel, woodruff

Stones: Jasper, lava, quartz, amber, beryl, bloodstone, gold calcite, carnelian, citrine, coal, diamond, geodes, red jasper, obsidian, peridot, smoky quartz, rhodochrosite, sunstone, yellow topaz

Metals: Gold, brass

Animals: Snake, cricket, lizard, bee, scorpion, shark

Season: Summer

Time: Noon

Tool: Athame

Signs: Aries, Leo, Sagittarius

Sense: Sight

Symbols: Flames, lava

Magic type: Candle, storm, time, star

Water

What do you visualize when you think about the element of Water? My first thought is always of the ocean, of waves crashing on the shore.

What would we do without water, it sustains all life. Without water we and all the plants and animals would not survive. Water is very powerful – the ocean, a flood, a tidal wave.

Water is all about emotions. Emotions flow, chop and change and rise to the surface as water does in a river, lake or ocean. A shower of rain can be refreshing like the release of emotion or destructive like the waves on a rough sea.

Water is also cleansing and healing. We clean ourselves, wash our food, and clean our houses and possessions with water. Your daily household chores such as washing up can be cleansing rituals in themselves.

Water is excellent for scrying. Divination with water uses our intuition, imagination and emotions. Take a bowl that has a dark coloured inside, fill it with water and drop a silver coin in the bottom. Calm and centre yourself, look into the water and see what images come to you.

Water represents the West. It is the season of autumn and old age. This is the time of harvest, a time to gather in. What we have spent the year nurturing and tending to is now ready to reap. It is time to let go.

As people get older and become more aware of their mortality, they seek to balance their lives. They surrender some of the hard work they have been doing and concentrate on what is most important to them. Often these are things that bring emotional fulfilment, like spending time with loved ones, or pursuing a creative dream.

Water gives us the flow of our emotions and nurtures our lives. In return, we can offer it our love. Everything we do with love, and every act of love we perform, honours Water. Love, like water, has the power of healing.

The colours of Water are the colours of the sea: the blue of the Mediterranean, and the grey of the North Sea; the black of a deep lake and the green of the sea before a storm. But also, all the glorious colours of the autumn leaves that remind me of the God Mabon.

On my altar a bowl filled with sea shells represents Water.

Direction: West
Nature: Flowing, purifying, healing, soothing, loving
Elemental: Undine
Colour: Blue
Places: Lake, spring, stream, river, beach, ocean, well, swimming pool, bath, shower, fountain
Magic: Purification, love, psychic awareness, dreams, sleep, peace, marriage, friends, emotions, subconscious
Herbs/plants: Aloe, apple, aster, lemon balm, birch, blackberry, burdock, cabbage, camellia, caper, cardamom, catnip, chamomile, chickweed, coconut, coltsfoot, columbine, cowslip, cucumber, daffodil, daisy, elder, elm, eucalyptus, feverfew, gardenia, heather, hemlock, iris, larkspur, lemon, lettuce, lilac, mallow, morning glory, myrrh, pansy, peach, plum, rose, sandalwood, sea weed, tansy, thyme, tomato, valerian, water lilies, willow, yarrow, yew
Stones: Amethyst, aquamarine, blue tourmaline, beryl, calcite, chalcedony, diamond, emerald, jade, jet, kunzite, lapis lazuli, magnetite, moonstone, obsidian, onyx, opal, peridot, rose quartz, rock crystal, blue topaz, pink tourmaline, zircon
Metals: Mercury, silver, copper
Animals: Cat, frog, turtle, dolphin, whale, otter, seal, fish, shellfish
Season: Autumn
Time: Dusk

Tool: Chalice, cauldron
Signs: Cancer, Scorpio, Pisces
Sense: Taste
Symbols: Shells, water
Magic type: Sea, ice, snow, fog, mirror, magnet

Spirit/Ether

There is the fifth element, that of Spirit. To me it encompasses all the others, but here are some basic correspondences:

Direction: All four – North, East, South, West and also within, without, up and down
Nature: Everything
Colours: Purple, black
Places: Space, vacuum, voids
Metal: Meteoritic
Animals: All and none
Seasons: All and none
Time: Eternal
Magic type: Religious

Working with Energy

To really feel magic, to make spells work and to get the right result from a ritual you need ENERGY.

Every living thing has its own energy, whether it is a flower, a crystal, a person or a pebble. All of the ingredients you might gather together for a spell will have their own individual energies and characteristics. If you use a wand, that has its own energy too, but the real energy comes from YOU.

Working with energy is really a combination, you can draw energy up from the Earth or from an item such as a crystal and you channel it through yourself, but you also add a bit of energy from your inner self as you do so. When you are in ritual you might also call upon the God and Goddess to lend their energy to your workings too, you can raise energy from other sources as well. The elements can provide us with energy too – Earth, Air, Fire and Water all provide sources of energy that we can tap into. But generally, you are also the conduit, you summon the energy, you gather it, you add to it and you direct it.

Everyone has energy within them, everyone has the power to access it, to tap into it and use it. Unfortunately, most people have no idea how to do so, and boy are they missing out.

The energy created by our bodies and by the spirit within our bodies is generally referred to as the aura. The energy that flows around and through our bodies is usually referred to as chi.

I would like you to try something now... yep right now... rub both your hands together (palms together) quickly for a few seconds, then very, very slowly pull them apart. Can you feel anything? You should feel a slight pull or a tingling sensation. What you can feel in between your hands is energy, that's the stuff we want to work with.

Another exercise to try is to hold your hands a couple of feet apart, palms inwards and slowly bring your hands together. You will hopefully start to feel a pressure as your hands get closer, a resistance – again this is energy. (Don't worry if you don't feel it at first, sometimes it takes some practice.)

Part of being a witch is to be connected to the Earth, her plants and her creatures, to be aware of the energies around us so that we can connect and interact with them.

You can form the energy and one of the most well used forms is the cone of power. This usually happens within a circle, the energy is raised by chanting and/or dancing in a circle, the energy builds and forms into an upwardly pointing cone that shapes itself in the centre of the circle and rises skywards. Once the cone is ready and it is felt that no more energy can be added, it is released and sent to its destination.

On a smaller scale we raise and direct energy when we work a spell, for instance a candle spell. We would take the energy from the Earth, channel it through our body and out through our hands and into a candle, this will charge the candle with energy. We add our intent and any other 'ingredients' such as herbs and oils. Once the candle is burning it releases the energy we filled it with, that energy then goes on its merry way to fulfil the intent that it was meant for.

Candle Magic

Candle magic is one of the most popular methods of working magic. It can be as simple as lighting a white candle and putting your intent into it or going the whole hog and tying in the correct colour of candle, adding corresponding herbs, anointing it with oil, carving runes or sigils, chanting a spell to go with it – or anywhere in between.

The choice is yours, it's a personal thing. Sometimes you may want to keep it simple, other times you may want to add to it – play around with all the various methods and see what works best for you.

What Type of Candle to Use?
Well, the choice is yours.

But for a candle spell you really want one that is not going to burn for days. Candles must not be left unattended, and for candle magic it is usually best to use a candle that will burn out in a short time. Tea lights are good, as are votives, small beeswax candles or even birthday cake candles.

What Colour?
A basic white candle is good and covers pretty much every intent. However, if you want to add power to your intent pick a coloured candle that mirrors your objective.

Here is a basic colour guide, but it is your choice – if a colour shouts at you to be used, go with your instinct.

Abundance – green, copper, gold
Astral travel – silver, black, purple, blue
Balance – white, silver, green, rainbow
Banishing negativity – black, white, purple

Binding – red, black
Blessing or consecrating – white, lilac, light blue
Cleansing – white
Changes – dark blue, yellow, white
Closure – black
Communication – yellow, white
Confidence – brown, orange, red, yellow
Creativity – orange, yellow
Defence – black, purple, white, dark blue
Divination – gold, lilac, yellow, black
Dreams – silver, purple, dark blue
Employment – orange, brown
Energy – gold, red
Exorcism – black, purple
Fertility – green, brown
Friendship – gold, pink, brown
Gossip, to stop – black, purple, white
Happiness – yellow, pink
Healing – light blue, yellow, pink, pale green
Love – pink, red, white
Luck – green, orange, gold
Money – green, gold
Meditation – purple, white, silver
Mental clarity – yellow, orange, white
Peace – white, black, pink, light blue
Protection – black, white, blue
Psychic powers – purple, black, white, lilac
Transformation – white, orange
Spirit contact – black, purple, lilac
Strength – red, gold, orange
Success – orange, green, gold
Truth seeking – black
Wisdom – purple, black, white

Carving

If you want to add more intent to your candle, you could carve a rune or sigil into it. Use a toothpick or a small knife and just carve your design into the candle itself. For instance, in a love candle spell you could carve a simple heart. Again, this is another area where you can go with what feels right for you.

Dressing Your Candle

To add even more power to your intent with your candle spell you can add scent to it, either in the form of anointing it with oil or with the addition of herbs. If you have a votive or small candle you can anoint it with your chosen oil (dip your finger in the oil and rub it on the candle from top to the middle and then bottom to the middle) and then roll it in ground up herbs. If you are using a rolled beeswax candle you can if you are very careful, warm the candle in your hand and gently unroll the beeswax then sprinkle the herbs inside and roll it back up again. If you are using a tea light you can add a few drops of your chosen oil and a sprinkle of herbs. If you have a glass votive holder you can place the candle inside and sprinkle the herbs around it.

Whilst you are anointing your candle with the oil and/ or rolling it in herbs, it is important to visualize your desired outcome at the same time, again adding to the power of your intent. By 'charging' the herbs and oils as you add them to the candle you are adding power to your spell.

Below is a chart showing some of intents and the corresponding herbs to use in your candle spells, as always, go with what feels right for you. Take a look through your kitchen cupboard and spice rack – see what jumps out at you.

Astral Travel – mugwort, dittany, poplar
Confidence – borage, thyme, yarrow

Divination – broom, dandelion, meadowsweet

Dreams – jasmine, marigold, mugwort, rose

Exorcism – basil, dragon's blood, frankincense, mint, sage

Fertility – geranium, mistletoe, oak, pine, rice

Friendship – lemon, passionflower, sweet pea

Gossip, to stop – clove, slippery elm

Happiness – lavender, marjoram, oregano, meadowsweet, St John's wort

Healing – apple, lemon balm, carnation, cinnamon, garlic

Love – basil, chamomile, clove, geranium, rose

Luck – heather, nutmeg, poppy, star anise

Mental clarity – mace, mustard, rosemary

Money – basil, cinnamon, marjoram, oregano, mint, pine

Peace – lavender, vervain, meadowsweet

Protection – anise, basil, garlic, ivy, oak, sage, rice

Psychic powers – bay, cinnamon, mugwort, anise, thyme, yarrow

Spirit contact – dandelion, sweetgrass, thistle, wormwood

Success – lemon balm, cinnamon, ginger, rowan

Wisdom – beech, dandelion, hazel, sage, sandalwood

Also use the elements – if you are using your candle for a spell involving emotions, how about a floating candle in a small dish of water, or standing a small bottle of spring water by the candle? If your spell is for grounding, stand the candle in some soil. Use your imagination, and go with whatever inspiration takes you.

If you work with tarot, how about picking a corresponding tarot card and standing it by your candle as it works its magic?

You could also add a small crystal chip to the base of the candle, pressing it into the wax.

Another idea is to surround your candle once it is in its holder with corresponding crystals, adding more energy, power and intent.

Below is a chart outlining some intents and the corresponding crystals to use in your candle spells, but, as always, go with your own instinct:

Abundance – agate, citrine, amazonite
Astral travel – sugilite, opal, jasper, hematite
Balance – bloodstone, rhodochrosite, yellow calcite
Banishing negativity – amber, amethyst, obsidian, tiger's eye, hematite
Blessing or consecrating – quartz, amethyst
Cleansing – mossy agate, amethyst, jade
Changes – snowflake obsidian
Divination – moonstone, quartz
Empowering – amber, quartz
Fertility – green jasper
Happiness – malachite, chrysacolla
Healing – sugilite, agate, selenite
Love – rose quartz
Luck – amazonite
Manifesting – sugilite, amber, kyanite
Money – malachite, pyrite, tourmaline
Meditation – fluorite, sodalite, snow quartz
Protection – malachite, dolomite, bloodstone, amethyst
Psychic powers – quartz, selenite
Transformation – amethyst, moldavite
Spirit contact – amethyst, black obsidian
Strength – bloodstone, diamond, mossy agate
Success – carnelian, citrine, malachite, aventurine
Wisdom – tiger's eye, ruby, jade, lapis lazuli, sapphire

Pinning Your Candle

You can also use a straight pin in your candle spell. This is where you place a pin into your candle at the spot where the magic will be released. Once the candle burns down to the pin and releases it the spell is done.

When Should I Work Candle Magic?

Well, again this is up to you. If you have a need to do the working right now... then do it. If you want to add a bit of oomph to your candle magic working then you could correspond it to the phase of the moon. The basic rule of thumb with the moon phases is:

Waxing moon is for growth and new projects.
Full moon is for completions, healing and empowerment.
Waning moon is for releasings, cleansings and banishings.
New (or dark) moon is for divination.

If you really want to get specific, you could also perform the candle magic on the corresponding day of the week:

Sunday – success, promotion, leadership, pride, light, fitness and personal growth. This is for achievements of any kind – fame, wealth, and acknowledgement. Health issues, increasing your personal power and sticking to diets all fall under Sunday.
Monday – inspiration, illusion, prophetic dreams, emotions, psychic abilities, travel, women's mysteries and fertility – well it is the moon's day after all.
Tuesday – bravery, honour, courage along with passion and strength to fight the good fight. Work on increasing all these things.
Wednesday – communication skills, cleverness, intelligence, creativity, business sense, writing, artistic talents, music, the arts and crafts. Seek the wisdom and improvement of your skills.
Thursday – prosperity, abundance, leadership and good health. Take the power of Thor's day and work with it!

Friday – well it is Freya's day so it's got to be love, fertility, romance and beauty magic, with happiness and friendship thrown in for good measure.

Saturday – Saturn's day, a God of the passage of time and karma. Saturday is a good day to work on protection, removing obstacles, binding and banishing negativity. Clean up day – clear out any problems.

Do I Need to Cast a Circle for Candle Magic?

Now I know you are probably fed up with hearing this by now, but it is your choice. Generally, I don't bother if I am doing the spell working at home as my house is regularly smudged and protected. However, if you are dealing with spirit, or negative energies then I would say it is a wise precaution. It doesn't have to be an elaborate ritual with quarter calling and bell ringing. Walk deosil around the area you are going to be doing your working in, visualize a bright, white light forming a circle, then forming a dome around you. When you have finished your working, walk widdershins around the area visualizing the protective circle dissipating.

What About the Spell Itself?

If you are good with words then a short chant works well, rhyming is good too. Make sure your intent is clearly stated; make sure it is worded correctly with no room for misinterpretation. I usually end my spells with 'a harm to none' just to make sure I am covered. Decide if you want to make it a long chant or a short one, a short one can always be chanted several times over. There are plenty of spells in books and on the internet; I have included some here as well. However, personally I feel that a spell will work much better if it is personalised for you. So, if you use a spell written by someone else, how about just tweaking it a bit so that it has that added bit of you in it?

Then What?

Well, you have got your candle, you have dressed it if you wished, you picked the day and moon phase (again if you wished), then what happens?

Set the candle in a suitable holder; place any other items around it – crystals, tarot cards etc if that is what you have decided upon.

Settle yourself comfortably in front of the candle. Take a few deep breaths to centre yourself. Light the candle and start with your spell or chant. As you say the words focus your intent in your mind. Visualize what you want to happen, how you want the spell to work. Send the energy of your intent into the candle itself.

When you have finished your chant and your visualization, leave the candle to burn itself out.

Now What Do I Do?

Take the candle stub and any remains of burnt herbs etc and dispose of them. Burying them in the garden is good. If you have used any crystals, it is a good idea to cleanse them – under running water, with salt or incense or however you prefer to do so.

Then let the universe do its work. However, if you have worked a spell to gain something you want – a job, a new love etc. You may have to do some leg work yourself. If you are after a new job but haven't actually got out into the world and looked for one then it's not going to happen. Even magic needs a helping hand sometimes.

I also like to give a little offering after working magic, even just to water the garden, feed the plants or leave some food out for the birds.

Candle Magic Prosperity Spell

What you will need:

A green candle

Optional herbs & crystals:

Jasmine or jasmine essential oil (for money)

Poppy seeds (for money & luck)

Pine needles or pine essential oil (for money)

Malachite (for money & success)

Green tourmaline (money)

What you do:

Dress your candle with the oils/herbs. Place it in a holder and put the crystals around the base. Light the candle and focus on the intent.

Say three times:

Lord & Lady help us to be

Good with finances and money

Guide us to financial good

Abundance, prosperity and guidance should

From financial worry set us free

And harm to none, so mote it be

Allow the candle to burn out.

Candle Magic Spell for Strength, Courage and Confidence

What you will need:

Red candle

Herbs/oils & crystals:

Allspice (courage)

Rosemary (strength)

Yarrow (courage)

Red jasper (negativity & strength)

Garnet (self-esteem & confidence)

Tigers eye (self-confidence)

What you do:

This spell needs to be worked on a Tuesday or a Sunday.
Dress the candle with the oils/herbs. Place the crystals
around the candle.
Say three times:
On this Mars day there is fiery energy to spare
For ...(insert name here)... I call for courage and self confidence
To know, to will, to dare
Three stones and a burning candle of red
I call for him/her, bravery and banish fear and dread
For the good of all, with harm to none
By Mars energy, this spell is done
Allow the candle to burn out.

Candle Magic Spell for Protection for Your Job
What you will need:

Black candle
Herbs/oils/crystals:
Rosemary (protection)
Ivy (protection)
Sage (protection, wishes)
Malachite (business success, protection, hope)
Jasper (protection)
Quartz (protection)
Tigers Eye (luck, protection)

What you do:

Dress the candle with the herbs/oils. Place the stones
around the base of the candle.
Say three times:
Crystals and stones of protection and power

Lend... (insert name here)... your strength and protection in
this magic hour
Safety and security this spell now yields
As we increase our energy and boost our shields
Health, wisdom and protection now do I call
In all seasons, winter to spring and summer to fall
For the good of all, with harm to none
By all the powers of three times three,
As I will it, then so shall it be!
Allow the candle to burn out.

Candle Magic Spell for Happiness

What you need:

A tea light or a yellow candle
Herbs/oils/crystals:
Feverfew (protection)
Red rose petals (love, healing, luck)
Yellow rose petals (happiness, success)
Rosemary (love, protection, healing)
Lavender (love, happiness, peace)
Rose quartz (peace, love, comfort, companionship)
Malachite (hope, happiness)

What you do:

Dress the candle with the herbs/oils. Take each stone in
your hand and charge them with your intent, then place
the stones around the base of the candle. Light the candle.
Say three times:
With the grace of Eros, Aphrodite and Freya
Please lift this grey veil of despair
Fill ...(insert name here)... life with happiness and light

To benefit them, family and friends with delight
An harm to none, so mote it be!
Leave the candle to burn out.

Candle Magic Spell to Deflect and Banish Negativity

What you need:

A thin black candle (a taper one)
An envelope or paper bag

What you do:

Sit in front of the candle and say:
On this day, this candle spell takes place
Fear and dread be gone, I banish you from time and space
Light the black candle. Visualize all the negativity and problems that need to be safely removed from your life.
Say:
This black candle represents all the negativity
With magic I break the bad luck that is surrounding me
Pinch out the candle flame and then snap the candle in half.
Say:
By the powers of the moon, the stars and the sun
As I will, so mote it be and let it harm none
Put the broken candle in the bag/envelope. Close it and put a drip of candle wax on it to seal the spell. Remove the bag from your property. Dispose of it. Once done, turn your back and don't look back. Put it all behind you.

The Crafts

Natural Magic Blessing for the Heart of the Home

What you will need:

Small dish of salt to represent the Earth and prosperity
Incense to represent Air and knowledge
A red candle for fire and courage
Small bowl of water to represent water and love

What you do:

Straighten the room.
Light the candle and the incense.
Place the candle in the centre of the room.
Begin in the East moving deosil work around the room; first sprinkle a little salt in each corner. Then carry the incense round waving the smoke to help it flow. Next sprinkle a little water around the perimeter of the room. Then settle in front of the candle and visualize the blessings from each of the four elements.

Prosperity from deep in the Earth.
Knowledge in the fragrant breeze from the Air.
Courage from the flame of Fire.
Love from the Water.

Picture these gifts and visualize you and your family receiving them equally.
Centre yourself.
Say this blessing:

Elements four I call, release now your power
As I bless my home in this magical hour
No negativity can enter, no spirit shall roam
As I consecrate and protect the heart of my home

As you finish the charm, draw a circle in the air above the candle flame with your finger. Spiral it up faster and faster, higher and higher, until you fling the energy off and out into the form. Then close the spell by saying:

This home is now blessed by my will and desire
I close this spell by Earth, Air, Water and Fire

Allow the candle and incense to burn out.

Spiritual Washes and Smudges

You and your home can attract all sorts of energies and vibrations, so I think it is good practice to routinely have a spiritual clear out.

It isn't just the magic that you work within your home that will bring in energies, everything that comes from outside will bring its own energies with it. For instance, your grocery shopping will have been held and touched by many people, each one adding their own energies to it, and they won't always be good energies.

So, Let's Clean House!

Salt is particularly good for spiritual house cleaning. Sprinkle a little in the corners of each room for purification and protection.

Smudging – this can be done with a bunch of dried sage, dried rosemary, dried lavender, sweet grass (or a combination) or even with your favourite incense. You can either start at your front door or in the centre of your home, but work your way around your house, going into each room and wafting the smoke around, making sure it gets into all the corners. You can use a chant whilst you are doing this, asking any negative energy to leave and to be replaced with positive, loving and happy energy.

Housework – yes, I know this is really boring. But the accumulation of dust, rubbish and mess in a home can cause negative energies. Clutter in the house can cause chaos in the atmosphere. You can clean out the negative energy by sweeping with a besom, sweeping from the front of the house to the back and sending out any negativity. You can even add a few drops of essential oil to the bristles of your broom to help.

You can make your own cleansing and purifying mist by using a spray bottle filled with distilled water (boil the water in your kettle and let it cool) and adding a few drops of essential oil to it and popping a rosemary, sage or lavender sprig into the bottle. Rose water, frankincense, cinnamon and lavender are all good for this purpose.

Once you have done the general housework you can use spiritual cleansers such as floor washes. These washes can also be used on worktops too.

All-Purpose Floor Wash

What you will need:

6 drops rosemary essential oil
6 drops pine needle essential oil

You can also add geranium or orange oil to give it a bit of spiritual uplift too. Or come up with your own essential oil combinations. Add the wash to your bucket of water and start mopping.

Florida Water

In hoodoo the use of Florida Water, an American version of Cologne Water, is common in households; it brings in good spirits and honours the ancestors.

What you will need:

16 ozs distilled water
1/4 cup vodka
6 drops lavender essential oil
2 drops clove essential oil
8 drops bergamot essential oil

You can also hang bunches of dried herbs above door ways to bring certain intents to the house. Rosemary, bay and thyme are good all-rounders for protection, lavender is good for a happy home, chilli peppers keep out hexes and cinnamon brings good spiritual vibes to a home.

Room spray – using a spray bottle and a base of distilled water (boiled and cooled kettle water) add 12 to 21 drops of essential oil to half a cup of water.
Some recipes ideas:

Chase Away House Cleansing Spray

1/2 cup distilled water
9 drops lavender oil
9 drops myrrh oil
3 drops rosemary oil

Soul Heal Spray

9 drops geranium oil
9 drops palmarose oil
3 drops lime oil

For Prosperity

Wrap up a silver coin and a basil leave in a piece of paper and pop it under your front door mat to bring prosperity into the house.

Cleansing the Spiritual You

The spiritual cleansing and blessing extend from the home to you with bath salt and sachet blends, herbal soaps, oils and waters. All can be made and used with specific intents.

Bath Crystals

2 cups (250g) sea salt or sea salt crystals
1 cup (125g) Epsom salts
1/4 teaspoon of essential oil – a combination that works for you, experiment.

Body Powder Base

2 tablespoons baking soda
5 tablespoons arrowroot or cornstarch
1 tablespoon ground orris root

Then add ground herbs and essential oils of your choice – dried orange peel, marigold petals, lemon balm, neroil oil, lavender buds and oils – use the herbs and scents that balance with your intent.

Four Thieves Vinegar

In 1772 during the plague, four thieves made a habit of robbing graves of the dead and stealing their precious items. As they came from a family of perfumers they knew the properties of herbs, so made a garlic-infused vinegar to rub on their bodies to protect them from the plague. Although thankfully we no longer have to worry about the plague, the 'four thieves vinegar' is useful for protection if applied to the body and for immunity when taken (1/2 teaspoon of the vinegar mix to 8oz water). If you don't fancy using the garlic you could replace that with an antibacterial or antiseptic herb such as rosemary or sage.

What you will need:

16 oz cider vinegar or white vinegar
4 cloves garlic

Mince the garlic, add a drop of the vinegar to it and mash until soft. Spoon the garlic into a sterilised jar or bottle and pour on the rest of the vinegar. Swirl daily for three to four weeks. You could make up a chant whilst you swirl, along the lines of sending evil on its way and keeping you protected.

Witch-Bottles

I love using Witch-bottles, I always have a couple on the go in my house for protection, clearing out negative energies and bringing happiness to the home.

Again, these are so easy to make, you don't need special pretty bottles you can just use old clean jam jars. Mine are in old jam jars so I tuck them away under furniture, but if you do have some pretty bottles, you could decorate them and make them a feature.

Generally speaking, the modern-day Witch-bottles are very similar to historical Witch-bottles in their basic structure, even though their intended purpose has changed. The most common purpose for constructing a Witch-bottle today is capturing negative energies targeted at the constructor of the bottle, her family or her home. Some Witch-bottles are intended to change negative energy into positive energy and then release it into the surrounding area.

The basic structure of Witch-bottles can be used for purposes other than protective: for financial gain, for helping with artistic creativity, to call forth positive energy, for improving health, etc.

Basically, a Witch-bottle is a container of some sort, usually a jar or a bottle, which is filled with objects that fulfil a given magical purpose. The person making the Witch-bottle or, in other words, the one casting the bottled spell, can charge the objects magically beforehand and build the bottle to work on this charging until the need of renewing the spell arises. Witch-bottles can also be built to recharge themselves by the energy they 'capture' for as long as the bottle stays unbroken, whether it is years or centuries.

The typical contents of the basic protective Witch-bottle today are quite similar to that of the traditional one: nails, sand or different coloured sands, crystals, stones, knotted threads, herbs, spices, resin, flowers, candle wax, incense, votive candles, salt, vinegar, oil, coins, saw dust, ashes etc. Actually, everything used in 'normal spells' can be used in this bottled version of a spell, the Witch-bottle.

Original Witch-bottles were used to keep witches away. They also used to contain all sorts of bodily fluids, hair and finger nail clippings – you can still use these if you wish.

Basically, start with your jar or bottle, then charge each item before you add it, layering up the ingredients as you go.

It really is up to you what you put in. I like to put in three nails to attract negativity and for protection. I also put in a piece of string with three knots in, knotting in my intent with each tie. If it is for prosperity, I often drop in a silver coin. I usually put salt in for protection, cleansing and purification. I also like to add some kind of dried pulse – lentils or beans to soak up any negative energy. Garlic is good for protection too. Then add any herbs, spices and flowers that correspond with your intent – rose petals for love, cinnamon for success, mint and basil for prosperity etc. Keep filling the jar or bottle up until you reach the top then put the lid on. If I am using a jam jar, I like to draw a pentacle on the lid. If I am using a bottle with a cork, I like to seal the cork lid with dripped wax.

If you are making the Witch-bottle for protection for your own home you might like to put in a pebble from the garden, a couple of fallen leaves from the tree in your yard and a bit of cobweb from inside the house, it makes it all more personal and ties the bottle to the energies of the home. This also gives me a good excuse for having cobwebs in the house. I need them for the Witch-bottles...

A Twist on the Witch-Bottle Is a Money Jar

Use a clean, cleansed jar and half fill it with rice or seeds (fenugreek seeds are good). As you half fill the jar visualize prosperity and abundance. Then every day add two more seeds to the jar, visualising prosperity as you do. When the jar is full bury the seeds whilst sending up a request to deity that your desire will be fulfilled.

You can also do this with a jar and your loose change, each time you drop a couple of coins in the jar visualize prosperity, every so often sprinkle in a few herbs that correspond with prosperity such as basil or mint. When the jar is full you can count it up and use it for something special. You can also decorate the jar with runes that symbolise prosperity and abundance.

Witches' Ladders

One of the most well-known charms using feathers is the Witches' Ladder. This is another all-purpose charm that can be worked in different colours, with different beads and charms added for different intents.

To make a Witches' Ladder, use three cords, yarns, strings or ribbons and braid them together, use colours that correspond with your intent if you would like to. As you braid, charge the cords with your intent, as you work through the braid add in beads, bells and charms if you wish.

59

The Witches' Ladder can be made to any length that suits you. Once it is finished, slip feathers in between the braids. As you add each feather state your intent. You can also slip pieces of herb into the braids too.

Incense

Loose incense is extremely easy to make. Start with a base, a resin is good such as frankincense or copal. Adding a wood of some sort helps your incense to burn longer too. Use something like sandalwood, or if you are using home grown dried herbs the woody stems of herbs can be added in too. Then the choice is up to you, whether you go for the scent you like or for the intent. Incense can be made for prosperity, love, success etc, but you can also make incense to correspond with the moon phase, a Sabbat, a particular ritual or to honour a specific deity.

I also like to add a few drops of essential oil to my incense mix once I have finished it too, just to give it an extra boost of scent and power.

Remember as well that incense put together for magical purpose may not always smell particularly pleasant, it is the energies of the herbs that are important.

I would also suggest keeping it simple. Too many ingredients and it gets complicated. Less is more as they say. So, pick you base resin and/or wood, tying them into your intent, and then add your herbs, spices and flowers – keep them corresponding to your intent. If you are making an incense to represent the element of Air you would choose herbs that relate to that element such as anise, lavender and mint perhaps. If you were making incense to honour the Goddess you might use lemon balm, geranium and thyme as these are all feminine herbs.

Don't forget that loose incense burnt on charcoal makes quite a bit of smoke.

Incense cones and sticks can be made fairly easily. Put together the ingredients you want and then grind them into a very, very fine powder. Make sure it is really fine otherwise it won't stick together. Then the choice is yours as to what you use to stick it all together, you can use gum Arabic, makko or tragacanth mixed with charcoal or saltpetre to aid combustion. (Please note that saltpetre is a toxic substance).

Incense pellets are easy to make, but again you will need to add something to help them stick together. Labdanum is often used (sometimes called neriko). Simply combine all your ingredients then add the labdanum bit by bit until it becomes a suitable consistency. Honey can also be used to stick your dry ingredients together to form pellets.

Here are some of my favourite incense recipes (use equal amounts of each ingredient).

Across the Veil Incense
Cinnamon
Honeysuckle
Marigold
Mugwort
Frankincense resin

Heaping on the Happy Incense
Basil
Fir
Lavender
Orange
Copal resin

Cleanse & Release Incense
Frankincense resin
Clove
Lavender
Cedar
Rose

Medicine Bags

Medicine bags, gris gris or mojo bags are fabulous to work with. (All different names for pretty much the same thing).

A medicine bag contains items that are charged with your intent and each item is a guide for the spirits to help them understand what the outcome you desire is. Your medicine bag once it is put together is essentially 'alive' with energy and it will need to be looked after and 'fed' with magic powder (instructions below). You will need to feed it periodically to maintain its energy force.

Africans call the power of nature 'ashe' and this is what is present in all herbs, plants and stones – in fact anything from nature. It is this power that we are using within the medicine bags.

A medicine bag can contain all sorts of items – herbs, roots, spices, crystals, feathers, bones, shells, dirt, pebbles, coins – what you put in your medicine bag is up to you.

I also want to mention here a hoodoo practice called Nation Sacks. This for women only (sorry guys). Men aren't even allowed to touch a woman's Nation Sack otherwise he will meet with bad luck. A Nation Sack is basically a protection aid for women and children. I think part of the power of these is the secrecy behind them. They are also sometimes used to draw love and can be extremely powerful, a love Nation Sack will often contain herbs and crystals, but will also hold hair, photographs and fingernail clippings.

I like the idea of a Nation Sack; I don't have one myself but I have a variation on the idea and use a medicine pouch. It is a small leather bag I made and I put things in it that I need at the time. It might contain herbs, crystals, a small bone, shells, feathers – anything that I feel the need of and I wear it when I am in ritual.

Traditional gris gris bags use red flannel for the bag itself, but I like to add colour magic to my medicine bags, I use orange material a lot as this is the colour for success, but also using green for prosperity, blue for healing etc works really well. You don't even have to be good at sewing, just use a handkerchief (do people still use these?), or felt is good as that doesn't need hemming, or just use a scrap of material. It can be tied with string or ribbon, but remember you need to get into it regularly to feed it. You can also use the chiffon bags that craft shops sell for wedding favours. Be creative...

Some ideas for you:

Fast Luck
Use green material for the bag and add:
Feathers
Nutmeg – for luck
A red lodestone
6 silver coins

Stay Away
Use orange or black material for the bag and add:
Rosemary
Pinch of dirt (graveyard dirt is good for this)
Pinch of dried dragon's blood
A black onyx

Love Drawing
Use red or pink material for the bag and add:
Rose petals
Lemon balm
Stick of cinnamon
Rose quartz
Sea shells

Magic Powders

And now on to the magic powder to feed your medicine bag, although magic powders also have lots of other uses. They can be used to roll candles in for spell work, to sprinkle around your house for protection, to add oomph to rituals and any spells, to add to poppets and Witches-Bottles or to wear in a small bottle as a charm.

To make a magic powder the ingredients you use must be ground so you will need either a pestle and mortar or the end of a rolling pin and a solid bowl.

As you add each ingredient to the bowl charge it first with your intent. I also like to charge the powder as a whole once it is complete too.

This can then be fed to your medicine bag each week, just a sprinkle; you can even boost the power by feeding it on the corresponding day of the week to your intent. Or keep it in an airtight bottle or jar to use for all sorts of other spell work.

I like to use a base for my magic powders. I usually use either salt or sugar, as it grinds well and adds its own qualities to the mix too. If I am making faery wishes powder I also like to add in a little bit of glitter.

A popular hoodoo recipe is for Hot Foot Powder; this can be used to keep enemies or bullies away and is good for protecting your property too.

Hot Foot Powder Basic Recipe

1/2 cup (65g) cayenne pepper
1/2 cup (65g) salt
1/2 cup (65g) ground black pepper

Use a suitable chant as you grind the powder together with your intent.

Sprinkle in the footsteps of your enemies to keep them away, or spread around the perimeter of your house to keep out unwanted people or thieves.

You can vary the mixture by adding red peppercorns, or chilli powder.

Fast Luck
Ground nutmeg
Ground cinnamon
Sugar for sweet success
Lemon balm

Stay Away
Mustard powder
Salt
Rosemary
Garlic powder

Love Drawing
Lavender
Ginger
Marjoram
Sugar

Offerings

An offering is easy peasey to make, you can use whatever herbs, spices, wood chips, crystals you want. Just mix them up as you would incense, grind to a powder if you so wish and then sprinkle on the ground by your favourite tree, in your garden, at the seashore – wherever you feel works best for your intent. You can also make offerings out of salt dough.

4 cups (500g) flour
1 cup (125g) salt

1 1/2 cups (350ml) hot water
1 tsp vegetable oil

Preparation:

- Combine the salt and flour, then add the water until the dough becomes elastic. Add the oil at this stage and knead the dough (if it's too sticky, add more flour). Once it's a good consistency you are ready to create.
- For offering balls, take a golf ball size amount of dough and make a well in the centre with your thumb then you can add herbs, whatever you have or want to add, you can tie them in with your intent. Then form the dough into a ball around the herbs. You can add a crystal chip into the top of the ball if you wish.
- A variation on this is to roll the dough out and use cookie cutters to make shapes, cut two shapes and put some herbs in between, moisten the edges with water and stick the two dough shapes together sealing the herbs inside.
- Bake in the oven at 200C until hard (about 20 - 30 minutes); keep an eye on them so they don't burn.

You can then use them as offerings when you are out in the woods, fields or at the sea as they are safe to leave outside, they are all natural and will bio degrade back into the Earth.

This dough recipe can also be used to make dough wreaths for the Sabbats, just separate into three and roll out into long strands, plait together and join into a circle. You can then cookie stamp out flowers or leaves and stick them to the plaited wreath with a little water. When it is baked you can paint and varnish it if you wish.

Ink

It is a lovely idea to write your spells and chants in your Book of Shadows with magical ink, and it is so easy to make.

You will need some coloured ink, red, green, purple the choice is yours. Then just add a drop or two of your favourite essential oil to the ink and give it a stir (not too much otherwise it will be too oily). You can also tie in the choice of essential oil with the intent if you are using the ink to write a spell.

Poppets

I know what you might be thinking – eeeek that's scary voodoo stuff. But don't worry, it isn't, I promise. We have Hollywood and the media to thank for that bad (and inaccurate press).

The use of poppet dolls in sympathetic magic is ancient, going back to the days of ancient Egypt. The enemies of Ramses III made wax poppets of the Pharaoh to bring about his death. OK that did involve some not very nice magic. but it wasn't all like that, I did promise, didn't I?

Ancient Greeks used poppets to protect against negative spirits or to bind two lovers together. West African slaves used poppets containing spirits to be carried with them as protective talismans.

Poppets are used in hoodoo and folk magic for all sorts of purposes, think of the poppet as a convenient and charming package for holding your spell, be it for love, luck, prosperity, healing or protection, for pretty much any use you can think of really.

Your poppet can be as simple as a few pieces of twine twisted together to form a stick man shape or elaborately dressed and decorated dollies or anything in between. You can make them from scratch using natural twigs, string, felt, scraps of material or you can purchase a doll in a store to dress up, the choice is yours.

I tend to make my poppets from felt. It is relatively inexpensive, comes in all sorts of colours, doesn't fray at the edges and is easy to cut and sew. I like to use felt because it means I can use colour magic as well, corresponding the colour felt I use with the intent of the poppet. I use a simplified 'gingerbread' man shape (as if he is standing with both legs together, so he has a head, two arms, a torso and effectively one big fat leg). Cut out two shapes (a front and a back). Sew a button for one eye and a cross stitch for the other, or two cross stitch eyes and a mouth. Cut out a small heart shape in felt and sew that on in the correct heart area. Put both sides together and sew round the edges, it doesn't have to be neat, and it doesn't have to be perfect. Leave a gap for stuffing.

Then you have to decide what to stuff him with. This will be according to what your intent is and to a certain extent what herbs, spices and plants you have to hand. So, for a healing poppet I might fill him with lavender, lemon balm and carnation petals.

I charge each herb with my intent before I use it as stuffing. Then when he is full, I sew up the gap. I charge the complete poppet once more with the intent and he is done.

The poppet can be placed on an altar, carried with you for protection or, in hoodoo, a poppet is often buried in the ground to work its magic.

Pendulums

All you need to make your own pendulum is a piece of string, ribbon or cord and something to hang on the end of it. A hag stone works well (a stone with a hole in the middle); a gold or silver ring works too, even a small piece of wood with a hole drilled through it.

Runes

Runes are easy to make. If you have access to the seashore, you can collect small round pebbles, all of similar sizes, and paint a rune on each one. They last longer if you give them a quick coat of varnish. You can also use the small round glass pebbles that florists use in vases, some of them come in really pretty colours.

Fehu – advance projects, used to send energy of other runes, temporary changes, material wealth
Uruz – enhances strength, sends courage
Thurisaz – breakthroughs, defence, change
Ansuz – wisdom, eloquence, inspiration, sending information
Raido – protection in astral or physical travel, getting something to move ahead
Kano – creating an opening, banishment, illumination, fire magic
Gebo – creating balance, healing, bonding energies, Air magic
Wunjo – wish rune, success, binds group energies in a positive way
Hagalaz – overcoming obstacles, banishing, blessing, defence activities
Nauthiz – seeking freedom, finding liberation, turning a bad situation good, turning away enemies
Isa – blocking negative energy, freezing a situation, finding clarity, binding negativity
Jera – harvesting what you have done, bringing rewards you have earning, improving a situation
Eihwaz – attuning energies, hunter rune, achieving true aims, finishing projects, closure
Perth – understanding a situation, initiation, secrets, vision questing, shamanistic work, fate
Algiz – protection, luck, defence, psychic abilities
Sowelu – bringing about victory, success, healing, making wise choices
Teiwaz – justice, honour, victory, order, courage
Berkana – starting a new project, fertility, purification, motherhood, reincarnation

Ehwaz – partnerships, overcoming obstacles within a group, psychic abilities with others
Mannaz – intelligence, career and school work, arbitration
Laguz – dreams, psychic phenomena, fascinations, glamouries
Inguz – focus, grounding, opportunities, calming
Othila – prosperity, finding fortunate influences
Dagaz – positive outlook, finding balance and harmony, transformation

Spirit Animal Stones

Each animal has its own characteristics and from those we can learn and use those skills and energies. Use an animal spirit stone to honour your totem animal, to use a particular animal's energies or to use those energies in a spell.

Spirit stones combine the healing properties of the stones themselves. A stone can absorb negative energy and convert it into positive energy, added with an image of the animal itself brings in the energies of that creature.

Use pebbles from the beach or from the garden, cleanse them and paint an image of the animal on, it doesn't have to be amazing artwork just a representation. Once you have done the image, charge the stone with the characteristics of that particular animal.

Magical Gardening

It doesn't matter if you only have a window sill with a pot plant on it, a small city patio, a playing field or several acres, you can always work with the magic in your garden.

Being in regular contact with your garden and what you grow, even with your house plants or a few pots of herbs, can help you to connect with the spirit of nature and recognise the subtleties of the changing of the seasons. Your garden can also provide you with food and magical ingredients.

Magical gardening does take time, focus and attention. You can't just plant something and leave it in the hope that several months later it will have grown, flourished and be covered in fruit or flowers (OK on the odd occasion it does happen, but not often).

Although I live in the city, I do have a small walled garden and I love it. I have some shrubs, lots of roses, lots of bedding plants in pots and hanging baskets in the summer, loads of herbs – all in pots, and several climbers. It is enough to keep me busy.

In the summer the pots need watering every day, the flowers need regular dead heading and towards the end of the summer I also collect a lot of seeds. The herbs need regular picking during the summer months, this not only gives me a good harvest but also encourages the plant to continue growing. I also dry a lot of herbs and flowers for magical use. In the autumn everything gets cut back and tidied up ready for the winter.

Over the winter months the garden pretty much looks after itself, I just pop out there to feed the birds. As spring approaches, I go out more regularly to tidy up and keep a check on the new items as they start to show their faces to the world.

The time I spend in the garden is a good way for me to connect with nature, with the Divine and to ground and centre myself at the end of the day. The garden is a good place for spotting the Fae. It is also the place I escape to when I need somewhere to myself.

My garden is where I stand in the dark to soak up the energies of the moon and it is where I stand in the daylight to soak up the energies of the sun. It is where my small chimenea stands that I use for any spells that require items to be burnt. It is where I go to meditate when it is dry. It is my haven.

I also believe that growing your own herbs and flowers to use for magical purposes adds some of your own energy into them before you use them in a working – a little extra oomph.

Harvesting and using my own herbs and flowers for magical workings also guarantees that they haven't been sprayed with all sorts of chemicals and pesticides too.

My garden is also filled with all sorts of things that aren't plants, I have beautiful wind chimes that help me when I meditate in the garden. I have a bird table and several bird feeders hanging in a small tree, feeding the birds not only helps care for the animals on this planet of ours, but I think it is also a way of honouring deity. I have pretty sparkly strings of beads hanging around too; these are there to look pretty, but also to attract the Fae. The back wall of my garden is painted with the shape of the mother Goddess and has sun and moon plaques hung around it.

From Outdoors to Indoors

The easiest way to bring some magic into the house or the home from nature's garden is with fresh flowers or a pot plant. Not only will it look beautiful and be a connection for you to the spirit of nature, but each flower and plant also has magical properties of its own that it can bring to your home.

Let's have a look at the properties of some of the more usual house plants:

African violet – spirituality and protection
Spider plant – absorbs negative energies
Fern – protection
Ivy – fidelity and fertility
Aloe – not only good to have to hand in the kitchen for burns it is also a plant of luck and wards against accidents
Ficus – love, luck, guards against hunger
Cyclamen – fertility, happiness and lust (a good one for the bedroom)
Pansy – to ease matters of the heart (folk name heartsease)
Carnations – health and healing
Marigolds – psychic abilities
Roses – lust, love and romance

With roses especially you can also add colour magic to the properties, so white roses would bring peace, yellow would bring happiness, orange would bring energy etc.

There are many, many shrubs and ground cover plants and all of them have magical properties such as hydrangeas, which are good for hex breaking, or lilacs and viburnum, both of which are good for protection. The periwinkle is a pretty ground cover plant that not only attracts the Fae, but is also excellent in spells for bindings, protection, love and prosperity.

But don't take my word for what magical properties each of the plants in your garden have, use your own intuition and 'spidery senses' to see what properties you think your plants have.

Flowers

Not only beautiful to look at and a source of nectar for the bees, flowers are incredibly special when it comes to magic. I think there are probably flowers of every single shade and colour – and again, here you can use your colour magic to work with them. Blue flowers can be used to represent the element of water, purple ones would be good for psychic abilities and power, pink flowers for love and friendship etc.

Of course, each specific type of flower has its own magical meaning too. Flowers also have a language of their own dating back to Victorian times, when the flower that was given to you by a friend or intended had its very own message – forget-me-not would mean 'true love', daisy would mean 'innocence' and thistle would mean 'I will never forget thee', although I am not sure about some of the messages personally, such as sage meant 'domestic virtues' and daffodil meant 'delusive hope'.

There are also flowers associated with each month, which can be used in your magical workings. Whether you use the correspondence to tie in with the date you are working the spell or the month of birth for the person you are working the spell for, it will add power to it.

This is a very basic guide to give you the idea, but again go with what feels right to you.

January – crocus, snowdrop
February – primrose
March – daffodil
April – daisy, sweet pea
May – broom, rose
June – lavender, yarrow
July – jasmine
August – sunflower, marigold
September – lily
October – dahlia
November – chrysanthemum
December – Poinsettia

Herbs

I think herbs are an important part of magical gardens. Even if you don't have a garden at all you usually have a window sill that can house a pot of herbs.

There are many types of herbs; some hardy some not. You will need to check which ones can grow outside and which ones suit your soil and area. I can't grow basil very well outside; it doesn't like our climate very much and I can't seem to grow parsley at all – but that is probably down to the folk tale that if a woman is in charge of the household parsley won't grow in the garden...

Deity

Lots of flowers and plants have associations with specific deities. If you work with a particular God or Goddess, you could put a plant in your garden that they would appreciate. For instance, cyclamen, willow and monkshood are associated with Hecate, roses and heather with Isis, violets and roses with Aphrodite.

Flower Fascinations

Fascination means 'to bewitch and hold spellbound', they are flower spells and charms.

If you put together the knowledge you have on magical properties within flowers, herbs and plants it is easy to put together a flower fascination. It doesn't need to be fancy, just putting together corresponding flowers and herbs with the same intent into a vase will do the trick. Put the vase somewhere that you will see it and visualize your intent each time you do.

Flower seeds can be added to medicine bags and charm bags then worn or kept with you.

Decorate a small besom or wreath with dried or fresh flowers with a particular intent in mind or to celebrate a Sabbat or honour a specific deity.

Keeping a dried poppy head in your purse for prosperity, tying a bunch of sage over the front door for protection, putting herbs in a sachet to keep in the car for safety and protection – all of these are simple flower fascinations.

Types of Gardens

You can also plant up your garden with a theme. You could dedicate the whole garden or a section of it to a particular deity and fill it with plants that honour and correspond to them. You could make your garden or an area of it into a garden for the Fae, the ideas are limitless really. I have seen herbs planted in a spiral to honour the Goddess, herbs and bedding plants laid out in the shape of a pentacle. A garden can be laid out in four sections to honour the four elements, each section having been planted with corresponding flowers and shrubs.

What about planting a planetary garden? You could choose plants that correspond to each of the planets, so for sun you might plant sunflowers, marigolds and rosemary. For the moon you might plant jasmine, pumpkins or gardenia. Mercury might be fennel, lavender and dill. Mars could be snapdragons, radish and holly. Jupiter might be meadowsweet, sage and honeysuckle. Venus could be violets, foxgloves and primroses and Saturn could be ivy, pansies and mimosa.

Faery gardens are very popular to create and can be very rewarding. You can create separate sections of the garden to attract different types of Fae, for instance a shady, earthy area for the gnomes and brownies. Generally, the Fae like water, shiny things and pretty, scented flowers. You could also place a few crystals in amongst the plants for them too.

Protection Plants

As most gardens are in the boundaries of your home, protection is quite a feature in the magical plant world. In the summer months I have a large trough at the front of my home filled with red geraniums as a protection ward. Ivy is also good for protection as are marigolds. These can be planted along the edge of your boundary or put in pots.

Meditation

I find meditation extremely important not just for my own inner peace, to relax and release stress but it is also a good way of connecting with the divine and getting answers to queries or insight into situations that you may have.

Try to meditate at least for a few minutes each day, I like to spend 10 minutes at the end of the day just to calm and centre myself and connect with my spirit guides, my totem or my patron deity.

These are some of my meditations I would like to share with you.

Spring Meditation

Make yourself comfortable. Take three deep breaths... in and out...

As your reality dissipates you find yourself standing on a muddy track, to your left are open fields, and to your right is the edge of a large forest. The sun is just starting to peep over the horizon.

The weather is cold and the air is crisp, but you are warm as you are wrapped up well. As you take a deep breath in you can feel the sharp air, cleansing and refreshing.

You start to walk along the path; the earth is hard and crisp as you make your way.

You can hear a noise, and you realise it is the bleating of sheep. As you turn round a bend in the track you see a whole field full of sheep and you notice that there are lots of lambs too, some are dashing about the field, others are snuggled up to their mothers. You stop and lean on the fence at the edge of the field and watch them for a moment. This is new life, new beginnings. Some of the sheep make their way to the fence where you are standing; you can feel their warmth and listen to them as they bleat to you.

Then you move on, continuing along the track. The sun has climbed up over the horizon now and its rays of light shine across the fields.

As you look across the fields you see movement, just catching a glimpse of something... you stop and watch closely... it moves again... it is a hare. She darts from one side of the field to the other, so graceful and beautiful. She is intuition and creativity. She leaps and bounds her way through life. A reminder to you that growth is assured if you are moving in balance with what is occurring in your life. If you move too fast or too slow an imbalance occurs and growth is stifled. Once she has disappeared from your view you move on.

As you walk you glance into the forest, there are still some last remnants of snow in the deeper parts of the woods, but you notice something else that is white, smaller and more delicate just on the edge, you bend down to get a closer look and realise it is a snowdrop that has pushed its way up through the foliage and the snow. The first sign that Mother Nature is awakening.

You straighten up and continue along the path... when... crack!... you jump... you look down to see what made the noise and find that you have stepped into a small puddle that had iced over, your foot cracked the thin layer of ice on top.

You can also hear the sounds of the wildlife in the forest, deep within the trees. The bird songs calling out to each other that the sun has awoken for the day. The small burrowing animals are starting to awake from their deep winter slumber.

The sun is now well on its way up into the sky and its light casts streaks upon the fields and glints upon the wet trees and foliage of the woods. But something catches your eye just inside the edge of the woods, a sparkle, and a flash of light. You make your way over to see what it is. As you look down into the undergrowth you see a small metal pot laying on its side, you turn it over and look inside. There, in the shadow of the pot, is a gift for you. You put your hand down and pick it up. This item is special to you; it is a sign of new beginnings, a new project perhaps, or a new direction? Take the item and put it in *your pocket, it already means something to you or it will in the near future.*

You stand now and slowly turn around in a circle taking in all the sights and sounds... the fields, the woods, the sun, and the wildlife. Capture this feeling, these memories, and take them with you.

When you are ready, slowly, breathing in and out deeply, come back to your reality.

Goddess Meditation

Settle and make yourself comfortable. Take several deep breathes in and out.

As your mundane world dissipates you find yourself standing on lush green grass in a valley between beautiful hills.

Breathe in the fresh cleansing air, feel it fill your body with love and light.

You turn and look all around you, in a full circle. As far as the eye can see there is lush green grass, interspersed with patches of pretty wild flowers. You notice at the base of one of the hills a glint of light, a sparkle – so you make your way towards it.

As you walk you can hear birds singing, it is a beautiful sound. You can smell the scent of the wild flowers on the breeze. You can feel the grass soft beneath your feet.

Your eyes catch a glimpse of the sparkle again, a flittering of light... or is it?

As you get closer you realise there is a large pool of water, it looks as if it comes in from the sea as there is a little sandy bay. When you reach it, you realise just how magical and enchanted the whole place looks. The sun glinting on the water, little dots of light flashing and bouncing off the ripples of water. Are they dots of light, or are they Fae?

There is a large flat rock beside the shore so you seat yourself upon it and gaze out across the water, taking in the beautiful scenery and enjoying the peacefulness the place brings.

You watch as two swans come swimming into view, gliding effortlessly and beautifully across the bay.

Then you hear a voice, singing beautifully. You stand and turn to see a woman walking along the shore to meet you. She has amazing cascades of dark brown hair and wears the dress of an Arthurian court lady. At her feet bounds a small rabbit, keeping pace with her steps. She stops occasionally to look at piece of drift wood or a pretty shell.

As she reaches you, she greets you and opens her arms for an embrace.

She then indicates for you to sit beside her on the rocks. She has an amazing presence... ethereal, beautiful, loving and caring but also one of strength and power. She talks with you, answers your questions, and shares her wisdom.

When you have finished talking, she embraces you once more and tells you that should you seek her wisdom or company again you have only to return to this enchanted place, and that the Fae will guide you to her.

She turns and you watch her walk away until she seems to disappear amid a cloud of the same sparkling lights you saw on the water.

You take one last long look round, drinking in the sights and sounds so that you can remember this place.

You then make your way out of the bay and back onto the grass, spread out before you.

Taking three long breaths; the beautiful hills disappear and are replaced by your usual surroundings.

Spiral Meditation

Close your eyes and take three deep breathes in and out. Releasing all the stresses and worries as you breathe out and visualizing bright white cleansing light filling you as you breathe in.

As you open your eyes you realize you are in a green field, the sun is shining and there is a warm breeze.

You can hear the birds singing.

You look up and see a small group of trees at the edge of the field and notice that you are standing on a path that leads to them.

You decide to make your way along the path.

When you reach the trees you hesitate, there is a quiet stillness about it, but you take a deep breath and step forward.

The air is cooler and the trees form a roof above your head casting shadows.

The twigs and leaves crunch under foot.

As you walk a little further you realize you are approaching a clearing. A few steps further and you step into shafts of warm sunlight.

You are standing in a sacred space in the centre of the trees.

The grass is lush and green and the clearing is edged with sweet smelling flowers.

In the centre is a large grey stone, you walk towards it.

As you near it you see there are some markings on it. You look closer and see that a spiral has been carved into the stone.

You run your finger over the spiral, following it round and round. As you do so you feel a tingle running up your arm from the spiral. As you follow the spiral round with your hand a beautiful cleansing, energizing light pours into your body.

When you reach the end of the spiral you take a step back – you feel wonderful.

You realize the sun has moved across the sky and dusk is settling in.

You make your way back to the edge of the clearing, turning to look back over your shoulder at the beautiful sacred space.

Then you make your way back along the path, through the trees and out into the field.

You feel refreshed, regenerated and ready to deal with any new challenges.

Taking three long breaths, return to your reality.

Paradise Island Meditation

Ground and centre yourself, take three deep breaths in and out and release all your worries and stresses of the day.

You are in a small boat gently making its way to the shore of a beautiful island. It's just you and your boat, letting the waves take the boat ashore. The sky is clear blue; the sea is a shimmering aqua. The sun is warm and welcoming. There are no sounds but the lapping of the water on the side of the boat and, as you approach the shore, the sounds of the waves meeting the sand.

As your boat draws to a halt on the beach you step out onto gorgeous hot, soft white sand and your toes are enveloped by the warmth. You look up to see a forest of dark green luscious trees in front of you, so you make your way across the sand.

There is a gentle cooling breeze bringing the scent of the sea and the taste of salt to your lips.

You step into the canopy of trees where it is cool and refreshing. Lush greenery covers the floor and as you gaze upwards there is a dark green sky of leaves. The air is warm and moist.

You can hear the sound of running water, not the sea but something else, so you make your way through the trees following the sound.

You come to the other side of the forest. Just by the edge of the trees, there is a cliff of grey stone in front of you with a small waterfall running from the top and splashing down into a deep, dark blue pool of water. You sit down on a rock at the side of the pool and dip your feet in; the water is beautifully cool and refreshing. So refreshing, you decide to go further in. You slide from the rock into the water; it is so cool and cleansing. The water washes over you, cool on your skin. You gently swim to the other side of the pool and climb out – you feel radiant, energized and totally at peace.

You walk from the edge of the trees out into the sunlight and back onto the beach, it is the same beach you landed upon, but you are further down, so you slowly walk along the soft sand, allowing the sun to dry you as you walk, feeling its warm rays on you. Back to your little boat, you climb in and push the boat off, back into the sea and head for the sun, which is now setting on the horizon. You feel refreshed and rejuvenated.

Taking three long breaths, return to your reality.

Tintagel Meditation

Sit comfortably; take three deep breaths...in and out slowly. Visualize all the stresses and worries of the day disappearing with each breath out.

As the real world disappears, you find yourself at the bottom of a steep street. As you look up in front of you, there is a tall hill with a steep winding stone staircase. The stairway is built of old, grey stone.

The hill is surrounded on three sides with the sea. Huge waves are crashing against the cliffs at the bottom. Seagulls are circling round, screeching and calling to each other. You can taste the salt in the air.

You walk towards the steps and start your climb upwards, taking each step slowly as the stairs are uneven and very narrow. With each step you relax a little more, feeling more peaceful in yourself.

The stairs wind steadily round and up, until you walk through a small stone archway at the top. This takes you out onto a flat area of grass where there are parts of grey stone walls, crumbled and abandoned. Lone rocks lie fallen; this was once a great and glorious castle... you have reached Tintagel Castle, once home to Arthur Pendragon.

The air is still, you can't hear a sound, not even the sea. It is so very peaceful, calm and quiet; broken only by the odd seagull as it swoops overhead.

You walk further onto the grass and turn to look out to your right. You can see the shoreline, the waves tumbling onto the sand and a large cave mouth... the home of Merlin the Sorcerer.

A warm breeze comes up from the sea; it winds itself around your legs, your body, your arms, and your face. You feel it clearing out all the cobwebs; blowing away all your worries, taking all your stresses with it.

The breeze brings with it faint voices... laughter, talking, the sound of a jester, horses braying and people clapping. You can't make it out at first until you realize it is echoes of the court that once was.

You can feel a tingle on your skin, but you are not sure what it is... until you realize it is the feeling of magic in the air. You can almost see the ghosts of Merlin's spells dancing and chasing around in the air. You can feel and taste the spark of ancient magic in the air all around you.

You stand for a moment, taking it all in.

Whilst you have been standing here, the moon has started to climb up into the sky, she is full and round and beautiful. You stand and gaze up at her. Breathe in her light until it fills your body with silvery essence.

You get a sense of love, of comfort and contentment, a feeling of having come home. Hold onto these feelings as you turn and make your way across the grass back to the archway.

You gradually make your way back down the stone stairway, with each step it brings you back to us, step by step, step by step. Down and around.

When you reach the ground you feel refreshed and renewed and full of ancient magic.

Taking three long breaths, return to your reality.

Autumn Melodies Meditation

Sit comfortably and start to relax as your world dissipates and is replaced...

You are standing outside a thatched cottage, the sky is a beautiful clear blue and the sun is shining, but the air is crisp and cool. It is a beautiful autumn morning. Laid out before you is a cottage garden, full of dahlias, chrysanthemums and geraniums. A gorgeous kaleidoscope of colours. Amongst all the flowers are vegetables and herbs; runner beans, courgettes, mint, rosemary and pumpkins.

It is so peaceful; you can hear the rustling of the trees, the leaves whispering to each other. You look up to see where their sound is coming from and realize that the entire cottage and garden are surrounded by a forest. There are tall trees of every sort, the light breeze moving the leaves. Shades of greens, orange and yellow are everywhere as the leaves have started to turn. You can also hear the buzzing of bees as they make the most of the last of the summer flowers.

Then you realize you can hear a bird calling, it's a wonderful, cheerful song. You stand and listen for a few moments and realize it is a blackbird. The sweet song of the blackbird, how wonderful – a blackbird can teach you the mystic secrets while in meditation. He can take you to a mystical place full of age-old knowledge and wisdom.

You walk further down the garden following his song, along the way you take note of all the bounty of vegetables that are growing in the garden. And also, the old foliage of plants that have given their all during the summer to provide their bounty and are now lying dormant, ready to blend back into the Earth.

At the end of the garden is a gate leading into the forest, you see the blackbird sitting on the fence post, but for a fleeting moment. In a flurry of black feathers and yellow beak he is gone... left in his place is one single solitary glossy black feather. You pick it up and put it in your pocket.

You turn and stroll back down the garden and as you pass through the door to the cottage you realize you are back in your own home.

You absent mindedly put your hand in your pocket and realize you still have the feather...

Come back to your reality.

A Starry 'Knight' Meditation

Sit comfortably, breathing in and out slowly. As you breathe in visualize a brilliant white light cleansing your body. As you breathe out, visualize all your worries and stresses fading.

Your everyday surroundings start to dissipate...

You find yourself sitting on top of a lush green hill. The sky above you is a beautiful shade of dark indigo and is filled to bursting with sparkling stars.

The night is still and silent. You sit there gazing in wonder at the stars above, and the beautiful full round moon.

Suddenly you see a shooting star sweeping across the sky... then you realize it is heading your way... you close your eyes as it appears to reach you, but nothing happens so you open them again.

You find standing in front of you a knight in gleaming silver armour sitting astride a gorgeous white stallion.

You can't believe your eyes! He must have arrived on the shooting star. As you sit there in awe he leans down from his horse and offers you his hand.

As if in a dream you take his hand and he swings you up onto the back of his horse and tells you to hold on.

He turns the horse and leaps into the air... you feel the rush of wind in your hair.

The horse gallops up, up, up into the starry night sky. You feel exhilarated as the knight and his horse lead you upwards, when you are so high up that you can almost touch the stars themselves, he levels out and slows to a canter.

The stars are so beautiful, as you pass by each one you feel each stress and worry that you carry in your heart and head diminishing ... one by one. Each star seems to be taking away your worries and replacing them with love.

Then you realize that the horse is starting to quicken its pace and that you are descending back down to the hilltop.

As you land the knight turns to face you and asks that you keep your heart and your head free from worry; that all will be taken care of – he asks that you trust in the Goddess to keep you safe.

In a blink he is gone – all you see is a shooting star heading upwards back into the starry night.

You feel amazing, light-hearted, hopeful and positive.

The hilltop and the starry sky begin to fade and are replaced by your own familiar surroundings.

Come back to your reality.

MOON MAGIC

RACHEL PATTERSON

PAGAN PORTALS

What People Are Saying About

Moon Magic

Don't let its length fool you; this little book packs a powerful punch. As full as it could possibly be with useful information and practical activities, *Pagan Portals - Moon Magic* provides a clear and direct interpretation of moon lore. Touching on a wide range of lunar-related subjects from moon-phase correspondences to astrology and Tarot, Rachel Patterson guides the reader through the practical aspects of rituals, spells and meditations based on the moon. The recipes for oils, incense and bath salts add depth and functionality to a book that is a quick read but that won't stay on the shelf for long; the person lucky enough to own a copy will page through it again and again for reference at every phase of the moon.

Laura Perry, author of *Ariadne's Thread: Awakening the Wonders of the Ancient Minoans in Our Modern Lives*

Moon Magic is a delightful treasury of lore and spiritual musings that should be essential to any planetary magic-worker's reading list.

David Salisbury, author of *The Deep Heart of Witchcraft*

Rachel Patterson has distilled the essence of everything connected with the moon into this wonderful and charming book. Moon phases, rituals, recipes, meditations, deities, power animals, signs, symbols, charms, spells, divination and so much more are tucked carefully within its pages and through it all shines the author's love of working with the moon and moon magic. A delight for everyone who gazes upon the moon and wonders how to work with its immense power

Yvonne Ryves, author of *Shaman Pathways - Web of Life*

Pagan Portals
Moon Magic

Rachel Patterson

MOON
BOOKS
London, UK
Washington, DC, USA

Contents

The Moon

A poem by Lesley Lightbody

Silvery light from the bright full Moon
Shining down, illuminates the room
Goddess in her Mother guise
Shines like a beacon in the skies
Soft the light shining from above
Like the wings on a pure white dove
Filled with hope and promise to come
Silvery light brings me home
Waxing, Waning, Full or New
The Goddess shines upon me and you
Illuminating our Path so bright
Follow the Moon and all is right

The Moon: Introduction

The Moon is such a beautiful sight in our skies; she is full of mystery and intrigue yet also full of immense power. She has been seen through history as being part of the occult and linked to enchanters, magicians and witches alike. Images abound of a wolf howling to the Moon and of witches flying on broomsticks silhouetted against her as a backdrop.

She is a huge part of all sorts of pagan pathways and plays a very important role in all areas of working magic.

Observing and working with the Moon and her phases is one of the ways we can tune into the here and now and the universe that surrounds us, learning to go with the flow of energy and follow her course. Working with the phases of the Moon also helps us to understand our own body and our inner thoughts, feelings and emotions. She controls the tides of the oceans; so the Moon is very much about our emotions which are linked to the element of water.

Within this book I hope to open up some of the mystery and guide you through working with her phases and to tap into her powerful energy.

We will start with the basics of the lunar cycle, the representations and correspondences of each phase, what magic to work and when. We will also take a look at the lunar year, Moon deities, Moon spells, meditations, specific Moon rituals, Moon names, tree Moons and Moon recipes.

Before performing spells and rites, it is a good idea to meditate about what you are trying to achieve and how. The phase of the Moon is something on which to reflect. Things can always be adapted – for instance a healing spell with a Waning Moon could concentrate on banishing the illness, whereas with a Waxing Moon it would be better to visualize increasing wellbeing.

I have purposely kept the wording within the rituals simple, but you can add your own words, deities and blessings to personalise them, they just give you a framework upon which to start.

There are several spells within this book, you can use them as they are or use your own instinct and intuition to tweak them to suit you, add your own personal twist to them. With all spell work the important part is your intent. Good visualisation, clear instructions and focus will all help to make your spell powerful. Please be very careful with your wording and your wishes, make sure you have stated your intent with great clarity as spells have a habit of working in extremely unexpected ways.

Please be careful when working with essential oils, always do a skin check. If you are pregnant my advice would be to avoid using oils totally unless you seek specialist advice.

Esbats

The word 'esbat' is believed to be derived from a French word
s'esbattre which means to 'joyfully celebrate' and is actually
quite fitting. The term esbat is usually used now to mean a
coming together of like-minded people to celebrate the phases
of the Moon with a ritual and/or spell work. It doesn't have to
be on a Full Moon or New Moon, it can be for any of the phases
of the Moon or planetary alignments and may involve teaching,
lessons or training of some sort as well.

The Lunar Cycle

Firstly, we need to understand the basics of the lunar cycle so
here is the technical bit:

The Moon has several cycles, but the one that is the most
obvious and that concerns us principally is that of the Moon's
phases.

The light of the Moon is reflected from the Sun. Although
from a more subtle perspective it is evident that moonlight has its
own special properties, the Moon herself has no luminescence.

The phases of the Moon are caused by the light of the Sun
being reflected in a different way, owing to the changing
relationship between Earth, Moon and Sun.

The phases of the Moon are the same all over the Earth. When
it is a Full Moon in Britain it is also a Full Moon in Australia,
China and the United States.

The passage of the Moon from New Moon to New Moon
takes 29. days. This phase cycle is called the synodic month, but
this can vary by as much as 13 hours because of the eccentricity
of the Moon's orbit around the Earth.

As there are 365 days in the year, most years have 13 New
Moons or 13 Full Moons, but never both. Occasionally a year
will miss out and only have 12 of each.

The lunar cycle can be divided and subdivided in a variety of ways because it's a cycle, and the different parts of the cycle naturally blend.

The usual way of considering the lunar cycle is to divide it into four – New Moon, Waxing Moon, Full Moon and Waning Moon – or eight with the addition of the Waning Crescent (or Balsamic), the Waning Gibbous (or Disseminating), Waxing Gibbous and Waxing Crescent Moons.

Within these parts there is continual variation, as the energies involved are perpetually on the move, growing and decreasing.

Why do we try to correspond our workings to the phases of the Moon? It is because corresponding magical workings to the phase of the Moon will add more power to them.

New Moon

We consider it to be the New Moon up to $3^1/_2$ days after the official New Moon. She rises around dawn, sets around sunset. Because she is between the Sun and the Earth nothing or very little is reflected and for a few days the Moon is lost in the brilliance of the Sun. When we cannot see any Moon in the sky, after the Waning Moon and before we see the first glimpse of the Crescent it is often referred to as the Dark Moon (see further chapter for more details).

As the Sun and Moon are on the same side of the Earth, the pull on us is the strongest. Because the Sun, Moon and Earth are all in a straight line this creates a time when the high tide is higher and the low tide is lower than usual.

This is a wonderful time to make new beginnings of all types. It is especially good for getting rid of bad habits. Habitual ways of thinking that are harmful and negative can also be abandoned at this time. It is also a good time to start something creative. New projects at work can also be launched.

The first day of the New Moon is really best devoted to the planning stages of ventures. It is good to feel just a little excited and filled with anticipation, although your energy may not be at its highest. A day or two into the cycle is the time to take the initiative, apply for that job, and start house hunting or any similar endeavours. It is also good for attracting positive energies, bringing about change, good luck and growth.

New Moon Colours
Green, white, orange and red.

New Moon Herbs, Oil and Incense Ingredients
Sandalwood, frankincense, copal, myrrh, rose, saffron, sweet grass, heather, patchouli, cinnamon, lavender, verbena, witch

hazel, jasmine, cardamom, cypress, ginger, nutmeg, orange, chamomile and lemon.

New Moon Crystals

Garnet, petalite, sapphire, quartz, labradorite, carnelian, charoite, peridot and phenakite.

New Moon Oil Recipe

4 drops patchouli essential oil
3 drops cedar wood essential oil
4 drops sweet orange essential oil
Add to a base oil such as sweet almond or grape seed (about 15mls of carrier oil should be about right).

New Moon Incense Recipe

2 parts copal resin
2 parts sandalwood
1 part dried rose petals
A few drops of myrrh essential oil

New Moon Meditation

Relax and make yourself comfortable. Close your eyes and focus on your breathing, deep breaths in… and out…Visualise the real world disappearing.

As your world dissipates you find yourself on a high cliff, behind you is a huge eyrie, the nest of an eagle. There is a light breeze, clear blue sky above you and the sun is shining.

You turn to face the eagle and connect mentally with its subconscious… Ask it to show you the pathways and opportunities available to you.

The eagle stands and stretches its huge wings, you realise it is an invitation for you to fly with him. Take some time and gradually shape shift into an eagle. Start with your feet, by morphing them into claws... then stretch your arms out and feel the feathers forming... your fingers changing... then your head slowly changing to form a beak... gradually you start to feel comfortable in your eagle shape.

A light breeze ruffles your feathers and your eagle companion makes ready to fly. You both perch on the edge of the cliff. The eagle suddenly takes flight... soaring across the sky... you take a deep breath... then leap...

Feel the air beneath you, feel it whisk around your feathers, glide on the current...

As you fly take a moment to look down, take in the landscape and the scenery as it rushes past. What you see while flying will give you insight into your options and pathways that are available to you.

Gradually the eagle leads you back to his eyrie.

You land safely on the cliff, exhilarated and full of ideas and plans.

At this point the eagle may give you a message...

When you are ready, slowly change yourself back from an eagle form to your own shape.

Then gradually come back to this reality, stamp your feet and wriggle your fingers.

New Moon Ritual

You will need:

A small plain white candle dressed with sage oil (or dressed with almond/olive oil and rolled in crushed sage leaves)

A goal you wish to achieve, it doesn't have to be grand

Cast the circle by saying:

Maiden cast this circle white
Free from shadow, pure and light
Mother cast this circle red
Cast any negativity from our head
Crone cast this circle black
Grant us the knowledge that we lack
This circle is now cast unbroken.

Call the quarters by saying:
I call to the East and the Element of Air, you who are mist and cloud, you who are fresh breeze and wild hurricane, Spirit of the Hawk, Spirit of the Sylph, hear me, bring into these rites, purification and clarity, sweep through and remove stagnation. Blessings and welcome!

I call to the South and the Element of Fire, you who are the crackle of bonfires, you who are the golden Sun and glowing lava, Spirit of the Phoenix, Spirit of the Flame Dancers, hear me, bring into these rites, your spirit of creativity and passion. Blessings and welcome!

I call to the West and the Element of Water, you who are the Undines of the rivers, and the sirens of the crashing ocean waves, you who are the Naiads of the Grottos, come to me. Spirit of the Shark, hear me, bring into these rites your deepest intuition and truest emotions, teach me to be flexible, to adapt and flow, like your waters. Blessings and welcome!

I call to the North and the Element of Earth, you who are bone and crystal, you who are tree and root and branch, Spirit of the Wolf, Spirit of the Gnome, I call upon you. Bring into these rites your spirit of prosperity, of stability and manifestation. Blessings and welcome!

Invocation to Deity. Say:

I call upon Vesta, Goddess of the home and the sacred hearth flame, join this rite today and bring with you inspiration and passion. Blessings and welcome!

It is the New Moon, everything is still, but there is a feeling in the air, a sense of something exciting, a building of energy and growth, new potential, new ideas and opportunities. The energy of the New Moon will guide you towards your goals; all you need do is put the ideas forward and into motion. The possibilities are out there and they are endless.

Look inward and find the beginnings of ideas, be prepared to set them in motion.

Now take your white candle and while you light it, repeat quietly to yourself what it is you want to achieve. It doesn't have to be a long-term plan; it can be something quite simple and basic.

Once your candle is burning brightly sit quietly and watch the flame. See how it fires and dances around, so much life, and so much potential. Ask out loud for Vesta to bring you ideas and new opportunities. Spend some time in quiet meditation now and let the ideas come to you…

If possible, allow the candle to burn out (safely).

Thank the quarters by saying:

Guardians to the Element of Earth, I thank you for your presence in this rite, I bid you blessings and farewell.

Guardians to the Element of Water, I thank you for your presence in this rite, I bid you blessings and farewell.

Guardians to the Element of Fire, I thank you for your presence in this rite, I bid you blessings and farewell.

Guardians to the Element of Air, I thank you for your presence in this rite, I bid you blessings and farewell.

Thank Deity by saying:

Vesta, Goddess of the home and sacred hearth flame, I thank you for your presence in this rite, may your flame of inspiration stay with me. Blessings and farewell.

Uncast the circle, walking widdershins, and say:

This circle is open but never broken.

New Moon Spells

I like to write a cheque to myself on the New Moon. I make it out to myself and write 'paid in full' in the amount box, then sign it from 'the law of abundance'. I fold the cheque into three and add three drops of peppermint essential oil on top after laying it in the bottom of a dish I keep on my altar, and then I sprinkle over it dried mint and lay three sticks of cinnamon on top. This works really well to keep enough money coming in.

At the very first sign of the Moon, just the slightest glimpse of her, stand outside and look up. Turn around deosil (sunwise or clockwise) three times and make a wish on the New Moon.

New Moon New Job Spell

If you have decided you need a new job, work this spell on the first night of the New Moon.

What you need:

Two brown candles (to represent your job)
One green candle (for prosperity)

One other coloured candle of your choice (this represents you)
Cinnamon oil
A talisman (this can be a pendant, a pebble, a shell, whatever you wish to use)

Put one of the brown candles in the centre of your altar with the green one to the right of it and your personal candle to the left of it. Put a dab of cinnamon oil on each of the candles.

Light the personal candle and visualise yourself working in the job you would love to do. Next light the green candle and visualise you earning enough money for your needs. Light the brown candle and visualise the company you would like to work for.

Leave the candles to burn out completely and send up a thank you to the Goddess/God/the Divine.

On the next six evenings light the second brown candle and let it burn for six minutes each time and visualise your goal.

When the six nights are up, if you still have some of the brown candle left, bury the remnants in the earth.

Lucky Charm

One of the easiest charms to use for luck is a hag stone (stone with a hole in it). These are found on many beaches and river beds. Leave the stone out on the night of a Waxing Moon, then thread a piece of green ribbon or cord through the hole and wear it as a pendant or hang it from your handbag, your altar or in your car to bring you good luck.

Saving Money Spell

We could all probably do with a bit of extra cash now and then in a savings account for emergencies. Money spells will always work better if we have a real need for the money to cover our basic living costs or specific essential needs rather than just wanting loads of cash to go on a frivolous spending spree!

What you need:

Three gold or silver coins
A green envelope or piece of green paper
Gold or silver thread
Moon water (or rain water works well too)

Hold the coins in your hand and visualise yourself with the money that you need to live on, or purchasing an essential item that you need or have to replace.

When you are ready, put the coins in the envelope or wrap them in the piece of paper and then tie the silver or gold thread around it seven times, visualising your goal as you do so.

Send up your wish and thanks in advance to the Divine and then knot the thread three times. Next, you will need to bury the coin package in the earth, somewhere in your garden (or in a pot on your windowsill) where it will catch the moonlight. Sprinkle the earth where you have buried it with the water.

Waxing Moon

The Waxing Crescent Moon occurs $3^1/_2$ to 7 days after the New Moon. She rises in the mid-morning and sets in the evening. The Moon's light is quickening. As the Moon has dropped back until she is about ?th of the way behind the Sun, we see her lumination as a crescent shape.

You will see the first quarter Moon from 7 to $10^1/_2$ days after the New Moon. She will rise around noon and set around midnight.

As the Moon is at a right angle to the Sun the difference between high and low tide is minimized. Because light and dark are in balance, the Moon will appear to be a Half Moon, but the area of light will continue to grow each day.

The Waxing Gibbous Moon occurs between $10^1/_2$ and 14 days after the New Moon. She rises sometime in the mid-afternoon and sets in the early dark hours of the morning.

As the Moon has fallen back around ? of the way behind the Sun, one side of the Moon is seen fully and the light on the other side bulges out, but does not yet fill all of the Moon's face.

Now your projects can get into their stride. Be aware, however, that overstrains are more likely at this time and that the body takes things in and absorbs them more readily with a Waxing Moon.

It is also a good time to build yourself up if you have been unwell or otherwise off-colour. Absorbing, boosting your energy and taking up supplies are crucial now. Go on an active holiday, get in touch with friends, plan a party, arrange meetings and increase communication.

As Full Moon approaches, notice what isn't working and shed it in order to focus your energies more effectively. Remind yourself to slow down a little and conserve your strength. This is a time of regeneration and to gather information and resources.

Waxing Moon Colours
White, pastel colours, red and silver.

Waxing Moon Herbs, Oils and Incense Ingredients
Coriander, geranium, juniper, marjoram, nutmeg, St. John's wort, tansy, thyme, caraway, mace, rosemary, rue, spearmint, bay, carnation, mugwort, pennyroyal, saffron, eucalyptus, cedar, hyacinth, ginger, pine, sandalwood, cinnamon and sweet pea.

Waxing Moon Crystals
Carnelian, citrine, aragonite, green aventurine, malachite, ruby and banded agate.

Waxing Moon Oil Recipe

6 drops lavender essential oil
3 drops basil essential oil
2 drops pine essential oil
1 drop nutmeg essential oil
Add to a base oil such as sweet almond or grape seed (about
15mls of carrier oil should be about right).

Waxing Moon Incense Recipe

2 parts juniper
2 parts cedar
1 part pine
1 part eucalyptus

Waxing Moon Meditation
Make yourself comfortable, close your eyes and focus on your breathing... deep breaths in and out... Visualise the real world disappearing.

As your world dissipates you find yourself at the foot of a hill, the grass is green beneath your feet and you can feel a gentle breeze on your face.

The lush grass is scattered with white daisies and you can smell their fresh scent in the air.

A small narrow track leads up the side of the hill in front of you, twisting and turning, spiralling its way up to the top, so you decide to follow it.

As you walk, following the path round and up with each step, release any stresses and worries that you are carrying with you…

Look out across the scenery, what do you see? What sounds can you hear?

Look out for any wildlife along the way.

Take deep breaths of cleansing, refreshing air as you walk. Walk on, continuing to ascend the path, heading always upwards.

When you reach the top of the hill you lay down on the grass, lying on your back and looking up at the sky. Watch the white, wispy clouds as they float past in the bright blue sky. What shapes do you see?

In the distance you see a darker cloud and realise that in the opposite valley there is a light rain shower, but the sun is still shining on your hilltop. After a short while a beautiful rainbow appears.

As you lie on the hilltop, allow yourself to draw renewing, invigorating energy from the rainbow, it is a gift from Mother Nature and she is happy to share it. Take as much energy as you need.

When you are ready, stand up and take a long look around at the landscape.

Then start to make your way back down the hillside, slowly following the pathway as it spirals down until you reach the foot of the hill.

Give thanks to Mother Nature and come back to this reality. Stamp your feet and wriggle your fingers.

Waxing Moon Ritual

You will need:

Two light blue candles, one white
Rosemary
Piece of paper
Quartz tumble stone

Cast the circle, saying:

Maiden cast this circle white
Free from shadow, pure and light
Mother cast this circle red
Cast any negativity from our head
Crone cast this circle black
Grant us the knowledge that we lack
This circle is now cast unbroken.

Call the quarters, saying:

I call to the East and the Element of Air, you who are mist and cloud,
you who are fresh breeze and wild hurricane, Spirit of the Hawk, Spirit
of the Sylph, hear me, bring into these rites, purification and clarity,
sweep through and remove stagnation. Blessings and welcome!

I call to the South and the Element of Fire, you who are the crackle of
bonfires, you who are the golden Sun and glowing lava, Spirit of the
Phoenix, Spirit of the Flame Dancers, hear me, bring into these rites,
your spirit of creativity and passion. Blessings and welcome!

I call to the West and the Element of Water, you who are the Undines
of the rivers, and the Sirens of the crashing ocean waves, you who
are the Naiads of the Grottos, come to me. Spirit of the Shark, hear

me, bring into these rites your deepest intuition and truest emotions, teach me to be flexible, to adapt and flow, like your waters. Blessings and welcome!

I call to the North and the Element of Earth, you who are bone and crystal, you who are tree and root and branch, Spirit of the Wolf, Spirit of the Gnome, I call upon you. Bring into these rites your spirit of prosperity, of stability and manifestation. Blessings and welcome!

Invocation to Deity:

I call upon the Goddess Athene, join this rite today and wave your wisdom and philosophy into this rite. Blessings and welcome!

It is the time of the Waxing Moon, a period of new beginnings, improving your health, attracting good luck, finding friendships, new jobs and making plans for the future.

Place the candles on your altar in front of you in a semi-circle shape, the white candle between the two blue ones. Place the rosemary by the white candle. Write the name of the person who needs healing or good health on the piece of paper and lay that in the middle of the semi-circle of candles. Place the crystal on top of the paper.

Light the candles then visualise the person in question in good health, happy and fit. When you are ready, send the energy from your visualisation into the crystal and through to the piece of paper beneath it.

The crystal can now be given to the person in question to carry with them for continued good health. The candle stubs can be buried in the earth along with the piece of paper.

Thank the quarters, saying:

Guardians to the Element of Earth, I thank you for your presence in this rite, I bid you blessings and farewell.

Guardians to the Element of Water, I thank you for your presence in this rite, I bid you blessings and farewell.

Guardians to the Element of Fire, I thank you for your presence in this rite, I bid you blessings and farewell.

Guardians to the Element of Air, I thank you for your presence in this rite, I bid you blessings and farewell.

Thank Deity:

Athene, Goddess of weaving, I thank you for your presence in this rite, may your wisdom and philosophy stay with me. Blessings and farewell.

Uncast the circle, walking widdershins (anti-sunwise) and say:

This circle is open but never broken.

Waxing Moon Lemon Spell

The lemon is ruled by the power of the Moon and works very well in this spell.

Use an unripe lemon, if possible, then using dress-making pins (the ones with the coloured heads work best). Stick the pins into the lemon. As you put each pin into the rind state out loud your intent, so you could put a pin in and ask for prosperity, the next one might be for happiness, the next for good health etc... you get the idea. When you are done, place the lemon on your altar, or you could hang it above your front door to bring positive energy into the house.

Waxing Moon Health Spell

Use eucalyptus on the Waxing Moon to bring good health and healing; use the essential oil on a candle, or burn the leaves in incense, alternatively, add them to a medicine pouch.

Waxing Moon Spell for Confidence

We all need a bit of a confidence boost every so often so give this little spell a try.

What you need:

A malachite crystal
A white candle
A green candle

If you would like to, you can dress your altar with white flowers and add some sprigs of green parsley.

Set the green and white candle on your altar and sit in front of them, light them both.

Take the malachite crystal in your hand and ask out loud for help from the Divine for courage, confidence and communication skills. Visualise yourself as being full of confidence. Touch the crystal to your mouth for the blessings of communication, to your ears for the power of listening and understanding, and then to your throat for the blessings of confidence.

Focus your thoughts on the candle flames until they burn out, keeping hold of the crystal as you do so. You can then carry the crystal with you in a pocket, purse or bag.

Waxing Moon Resolution Spell

Sometimes, when we have resolved to do something or stick to a regime, our resolution wavers. This spell will help strengthen it.

You will need:

A purple candle
White thread

Start by winding the cotton three times deosil (clockwise) around the candle, about a third of the way down. As you do so, focus on your breathing, taking deep breaths in and out. On the third wrap of the cotton take a deep breath in and hold it for a count of six. Visualise yourself being surrounded in purple light to give you strength.

When you are ready, light the candle and focus on the flame. As you do so, ask out loud for strength in your resolve and help with keeping your focus on the task. End with the words *'and harm to none, so mote it be'*.

Crescent Moon Cookies

These are lovely to make to eat during (or after... or both) your Moon ritual.

You will need:

$1^1/_2$ cups (190g) all purpose (plain) flour
$1^1/_2$ teaspoons baking soda
$1^1/_2$ teaspoons baking powder
1 cup (225g) butter (softened)
$2^1/_2$ cups (375g) sugar
1 egg
1 teaspoon vanilla extract

- Preheat the oven to 350 degrees.
- Cream the butter and sugar together until the mixture is light and creamy.
- Add the egg, butter and sugar and mix them together well.
- In a separate bowl mix together the flour, baking powder and baking soda.

- Then gradually add the dry ingredient mix to the wet ingredients, mix until it becomes dough.
- Flour your hands and roll the dough into small ball shapes (about the size of a golf ball). Flatten each ball shape down and make it into a crescent shape. You can also just roll the dough out and use crescent shape cookie cutters (you will need to flour the cutter before each use so it doesn't stick).
- Bake the biscuits on an ungreased baking tray for about ten minutes.

Crescent Moon Magic

This is magic worked as the Moon rises at mid-morning and sets after sunset. It is good for animals, business, change, emotions, matriarchal strength. This phase of the Moon represents zest of life with the aid of stability. It helps bring forth courage and optimism.

Gibbous Moon Magic

The Gibbous Moon is almost full, but not completely full. The magic of this phase is good for patience, purity and protection. It creates atmosphere for meditation and centring. It can symbolise innocence.

Full Moon

About 15 days after the after the New Moon, the Full Moon first appears. At this point the Moon is on the opposite side of the Earth from the Sun, so she rises around sunset and sets around dawn.

The Sun shines fully on her face and tides are at their extremes again. Some may sense the pull of the Sun from one direction, and the Moon from the opposite, and their energy will feel a bit scattered.

Hold a party or an event, but be aware that the energy level is likely to be high and anything troublesome is likely to surface. Cook and stock up the freezer. Pay special attention to your creative ventures and your dreams.

This is a good time to try out forms of divinations such as scrying or tarot. Reflect about your goals, feelings and matters that have to do with relationship and family. It is also good for transformations, psychic abilities, strength, love, power and fertility.

The Full Moon is also an excellent time to cleanse, purify and charge your crystals. Lay them out so that the moonlight can hit them; if you can do so safely, leave them outside. If not, find a windowsill that catches the moonlight. Don't just stop at crystals though, your magical tools will also benefit from soaking up the power of the moonlight.

As the Full Moon just passes, the time arrives to put the finishing touches on what you have been doing and to get ready for the quieter time to come. Enjoy beauty and art, listen to music. If you have argued with someone but do not feel the issues are really vital, make up now.

If you live near the sea the Full Moon is a wonderful time to visit the shoreline and (if safe and legal to do so) build a small fire. Collect small pieces of driftwood to build your fire and, as you lay each piece onto the fire, add a wish. Once the fire is burning nicely, cast offerings into the flames as gifts to the Moon Goddess, such as herbs, flowers and leaves. Sit and watch as the fire burns. If you don't live near the sea, you could turn this into a visualisation for a Full Moon meditation.

Full Moon Colours
Blue, white, yellow and orange.

Full Moon Herbs, Oils and Incense Ingredients
Frankincense, sandalwood, rose, cedar, juniper berry, hyssop, myrtle, orange, rosewood, tangerine, tea tree, yarrow and sage.

Full Moon Crystals
Moonstone, selenite, quartz, black tourmaline, obsidian, amber, rose quartz and opal.

Full Moon Oil Recipe

6 drops gardenia essential oil
4 drops lotus essential oil
2 drops jasmine essential oil
Add to a base oil such as sweet almond or grape seed (about
15mls of carrier oil should be about right)

Full Moon Balm (for pulse points)

6 drops sandalwood essential oil
3 drops lemon essential oil
2 drops palma rose essential oil
1/4 cup grated beeswax
1/4 cup vegetable oil

Melt oil and wax together, cool slightly then stir in essential oils. Store in an airtight pot.

Full Moon Incense (loose mix to burn on charcoal disc)

2 parts sandalwood
2 parts frankincense resin
1/4 part dried rose petals
1/2 part orris root
6 drops sandalwood oil

Moon Magic Bath Salts

1 cup sea salt
8 drops sandalwood essential oil
8 drops lotus essential oil

Mix together and store in an airtight container, sprinkle a couple of tablespoons of the mixture in your bath.

Full Moon Meditation

Relax and make yourself comfortable, close your eyes and focus on your breathing, deep breaths in and out... Visualise the real word disappearing.

As your world dissipates you find yourself on the edge of a forest. It is night-time and the sky is a deep, dark blue, but it is scattered with thousands of sparkling stars and the Moon is full and bright, bright enough to light your way.

You enter the forest between two yew trees, the air is cool and you can smell the earthy scent of the forest floor. There appears to be a small pathway between the trees, which you start to follow. The leaves crackle under foot and you can hear the sounds of birds and wildlife above and all around you.

You follow the path until it leads to a clearing. As you leave the trees you step into dappled sunlight… in the centre of the clearing is a deep pool of water, the surface of which is perfectly still.

You walk right up to the edge of the pool and sit down beside it.

As you gaze into the water you realise the Full Moon above you is reflected onto the surface of the dark water.

You put your hand down and trail your fingers through the water which sends ripples across the surface.

You centre your thoughts and think of a question or situation you need an answer or clarity to…

Look to the surface of the water for signs and symbols… what do you see? Above you a hoot sounds out across the woods and, with a flapping of wings, a huge owl takes flight from a tree above you and flies across the clearing.

When you have finished your scrying stand up and make your way back to the pathway and head to the edge of the forest.

Slowly bring yourself back to this reality, stamp your feet and wriggle your fingers.

Full Moon Ritual

You will need:

A cauldron (or dish with a dark inside) half filled with water
A small silver coin

Cast the circle, saying:

Maiden cast this circle white
Free from shadow, pure and light
Mother cast this circle red
Cast any negativity from our head
Crone cast this circle black

Grant us the knowledge that we lack
This circle is now cast unbroken.

Call the quarters, saying:

I call to the East and the Element of Air, you who are mist and cloud,
you who are fresh breeze and wild hurricane, Spirit of the Hawk, Spirit
of the Sylph, hear me, bring into these rites, purification and clarity,
sweep through and remove stagnation. Blessings and welcome!

I call to the South and the Element of Fire, you who are the crackle of
bonfires, you who are the golden Sun and glowing lava, Spirit of the
Phoenix, Spirit of the Flame Dancers, hear me, bring into these rites,
your spirit of creativity and passion. Blessings and welcome!

I call to the West and the Element of Water, you who are the Undines of
the rivers, and the Sirens of the crashing ocean waves, you who are the
Naiads of the Grottos, come to me. Spirit of the Shark, hear me, bring
into these rites your deepest intuition and truest emotions, teach me to
be flexible, to adapt and flow, like your waters. Blessings and welcome!

I call to the North and the Element of Earth, you who are bone and
crystal, you who are tree and root and branch, Spirit of the Wolf,
Spirit of the Gnome, I call upon you. Bring into these rites your spirit
of prosperity, of stability and manifestation. Blessings and welcome!

Invocation to Deity:

I call upon Yemaya, Goddess of the seas, join this rite today and bring
with your feminine energy and healing. Blessings and welcome!

The Full Moon is a powerful time; she carries with her magic
to aid in immediate need, power boosts, courage, psychic

protection and healing. This Moon phase can also bring urgently needed money, commitment, justice and ambition.

Sit quietly in front of your cauldron of water and drop a silver coin into the water, if you can position the cauldron so that the moonlight reflects into it even better. You can gather the Moon's energy by skimming your hand just across the top of the water.

Say a chant to the Goddess and the Full Moon asking for enough money to cover your needs. Visualise the goal.

Leave the water and the coin in the cauldron until the following day when you can tip the water onto the earth.

Thank the quarters, saying:

Guardians to the Element of Earth, I thank you for your presence in this rite, I bid you blessings and farewell.

Guardians to the Element of Water, I thank you for your presence in this rite, I bid you blessings and farewell.

Guardians to the Element of Fire, I thank you for your presence in this rite, I bid you blessings and farewell.

Guardians to the Element of Air, I thank you for your presence in this rite, I bid you blessings and farewell.

Thank Deity:

Goddess Yemaya, I thank you for your presence in this rite, may your energy and healing stay with me. Blessings and farewell.

Uncast the circle, walking widdershins, saying:

This circle is open but never broken.

Making Moon Water

Moon water is really simple to make and can be used for all sorts of spell work, rituals and anointing. It is useful to have in stock when you need to use the power of the Moon phase at a different time.

Using a dish, bowl or bottle, fill it with spring water and leave it outside (if it can be safely done) or on a windowsill so that it can soak up the power of the Full Moon. You can also do the same process on the New, Waxing, Waning or Dark Moon phases too. Once the water has absorbed the power of the Moon, you can keep it in an airtight bottle for future use.

You can also add a pinch of sea salt to the water to give it extra cleansing and purifying oomph.

Camellia Money Spell

I have a beautiful camellia bush in my garden that is covered with pink blossoms. I pick up the flowers once they have dropped on the ground in spring and place them on my altar, as they stay in perfect condition for several days afterwards.

The camellia brings riches and luxury, and so is used in spells of this kind.

Place the blossoms in vessels of water on your altar during money and prosperity rituals, or use them in spells.

The lovely Moon-ruled blooms of the Camellia are ideal for money spells. Just before Full Moon, place a bowl of them on your altar and drop three silver coins in between the blooms, naming one for money to spend, one for a loved one to spend it on and the third for the wisdom to spend it wisely. When your rite is over, take the three coins and keep them in a piece of cotton. Press one of the flowers between two sheets of tissue paper and keep that with the coins as your fortune begins to grow.

When casting Full Moon spells, it is best to go outside during the night of a Full Moon. Go to a location where you will not be disturbed. Face the direction of the Moon.

Full Moon Wish Spell

Take a couple of pennies and go outside where you can clearly see the Full Moon. Hold the pennies in your hand and ask out loud that your wish be granted. Visualise what your goal is... and state it out loud. Throw the pennies up into the air towards the Moon. Then say out loud that you offer the pennies to the Moon and give thanks.

Lemon Balm for Love

Lemon balm grows like a wild thing in my garden, so much so that I have had to contain it in pots! It is a plant that is ruled by the Moon.

For this spell soak a few lemon balm leaves in apple juice (also a fruit of love), leave the mixture in a place where it can capture the light of the Full Moon then share the drink with your partner using the same cup, this should ensure a strong and true love.

Arianrhod's Silver Wheel Divination

This is a fun project to make and do. Be creative and go with your instincts on what materials to use.

Take a piece of square cloth, you will need to draw a circle in the centre of it (or sew, embroider – whatever skills you have!) Then mark the circle into quarters. Within the centre of each circle draw (or sew) a phase of the Moon – a black circle for the Dark Moon, a crescent for the Waxing Moon, a white circle for the Full Moon and a crescent for the Waning Moon. (Drawing around a coin might help keep the circles an even shape).

Next you will need 13 stones. You can either use tumble stone crystals that you might already have, or purchase them specifically for this or collect natural pebbles from the beach or riverbed.

You will need to identify each stone, so coloured tumble stone crystals are easier, but you could mark natural pebbles as well, preferably three red, three green, three blue, three brown and one black. A bag is useful to keep them all in.

You can go with your own meanings and correspondences for each stone or each colour group but a good guideline is:

- Red stones represent energy, career and the future.
- Blue stones represent mental energy, communication, thoughts, study and the present.
- Green stones represent healing, love, family and the past.
- Brown stones represent money, physical body, practical things and the very distant past.
- The black stone is the unknown, surprises and mysteries.

When you have all your items ready, ground and centre yourself, then form a question in your mind. Draw a stone from the bag without looking at it, hold your hand above the cloth and let the stone fall. Repeat this process three times. If the stone falls outside the circle on the cloth, then it is disregarded.

The first stone you cast surrounds your situation, the second stone represents current conditions and the third stone is the outcome. If you aren't clear on the reading, you can draw a fourth stone for clarification.

Depending on which quarter of the circle the stone drops in will bear relation to the colour of the stone, and therefore, the answer to your question. Use the meanings of the phases of the Moon to relate to the stone, so the Waxing Moon segment would mean revealing or growth.

Go with your intuition!

Disseminating Moon Magic

This is when the Moon is just past being full, and appears slightly flat on one side. This phase is good for addictions, decisions, divorce, emotions, stress, and protection. It builds knowledge, sharing, calming, vocal expression and communication. The Disseminating Moon also aids meditation and enhances inner attunement.

Waning Moon

The Waning Gibbous Moon or Disseminating Moon appears $3^1/_2$ days to 7 days after the Full Moon. The Moon will rise during the evening and set sometime mid-morning. Again, we see the bulge on one side of the Moon but it is now decreasing each day. Darkness is slowly moving in. Waning is underway.

The Waning Last Quarter Moon appears between 7 and $10^1/_2$ days after the Full Moon. She rises near midnight and sets near noon. Because of the return to a right angle between the Sun and Moon the variation between tides is low again. There is once again a balance between light and dark, but the dark will soon overcome the light.

The Waning Crescent or Balsamic Moon occurs between $10^1/_2$ days after the Full Moon up until the New Moon. The Moon rises in the dark hours of the morning and sets in the afternoon. Again, we see the Moon as a beautiful crescent, but it is rapidly diminishing into darkness.

You do not have to be concerned so much about overdoing things now because the lunar rhythm will act as something of a brake. Now is a good time to throw away your rubbish, take old clothes to charity shops. Consider how well things are working out and analyse information. Follow your needs and reactions.

You may feel more like meditating and being alone. Clear spaces of all descriptions and make endings, let go of unwanted energies, release, banish and reverse. Some people favour scrying and meditation with the Dark Moon because it is a more inward time. The insights you glean now will have a deeper more insightful quality, whereas as Full Moon they may be more obviously creative.

To connect with the Waxing Moon energies and the energy of the Crone, place an amethyst in a bowl of water, light a purple candle and scry.

Use a hag stone (holey stone) or a piece of elder or yew wood. Hold this during meditation to connect with crone energies and the energy of the Waning Moon.

Make a crone hearth in your fireplace or on your mantelpiece. Decorate it with symbols that represent her to you, or you could just use a cauldron (or big casserole dish) and fill it with a large dark coloured candle and pebbles.

Waning Moon Colours

Blue, purple and pink.

Waning Moon herbs, Oils and Incense Ingredients

Anise, bay, eucalyptus, cypress, frankincense, hyssop, jasmine, lime, marjoram, myrtle, orange, sandalwood, tangerine, tea tree, sage, lavender and yarrow.

Waning Moon Crystals

Smokey quartz, rhodochrosite, rose quartz, rhodonite, ruby in fuchsite, pink kunzite and danburite.

Waning Moon Bath Salts

1 cup sea salt
3 drops geranium essential oil
3 drops pine essential oil
6 drops magnolia essential oil

Waning Moon Oil Recipe

4 drops cypress essential oil
3 drops clove essential oil
3 drops cedar wood essential oil
Add to a base oil such as sweet almond or grape seed (about 15mls of carrier oil should be about right).

Waning Moon Incense Recipe

3 parts frankincense resin

2 parts myrrh

1 part sandalwood

A few drops of sandalwood essential oil

Make a Crone Circlet

This is lovely to wear during a Waning Moon ritual. Take a base of wire and add leaves, flowers and twigs. Use dark coloured ribbon, such as dark purples, blues and black, to decorate it. As you make the circlet add in the intent of your dreams and wishes that you wish to fulfil.

Waning Moon Meditation

Relax and make yourself comfortable, close your eyes and focus on your breathing, deep breaths in... and out... Visualise the real world disappearing.

As your world dissipates you find yourself on a beach. The waves are crashing onto the shore in front of you and you can smell the salt in the air. As you turn around there is a rocky landscape behind you. As you look you can see a gap between the rocks so you go to investigate. You squeeze through the gap and find yourself in a passageway of rocks.

As you follow the corridor of rock it suddenly opens out into a small paradise scene. You are surrounded by palm trees and in front of you is a huge waterfall. The sound of the water is very loud but beautiful. You can feel the power of it in your chest.

Make your way to the edge of the waterfall... as you get closer you can just make out a cave behind the curtain of water.

You suddenly feel the urge to step into the cascading water. You step carefully and end up standing directly below the waterfall. It is cool and refreshing.

As you allow the water to fall over you, let go of old habits, negative energies and anything that does not serve your higher good. Let the water wash it all away.

When you are finished you feel refreshed and renewed.

Step back out of the cascading water and sit down beside it. Now take some time to think about all the positive things in your life, fill your mind with happy thoughts and new goals.

Then stand up and make your way back to the passageway through the rocks and back out to the shore.

Take a moment to watch the waves and when you are ready come back to this reality, stamp your feet and wriggle your toes.

Waning Moon Ritual

You will need:

Large leaf herbs that you associate with the Moon (see list below).

A dark candle

Soak a pinch of the herbs in a bowl of salt water overnight if possible. Then remove them from the water and leave them to dry.

Cast the circle, saying:

Maiden cast this circle white
Free from shadow, pure and light
Mother cast this circle red
Cast any negativity from our head
Crone cast this circle black
Grant us the knowledge that we lack
This circle is now cast unbroken.

Call the quarters, saying:

I call to the East and the Element of Air, you who are mist and cloud, you who are fresh breeze and wild hurricane, Spirit of the Hawk, Spirit of the Sylph, hear me, bring into these rites, purification and clarity, sweep through and remove stagnation. Blessings and welcome!

I call to the South and the Element of Fire, you who are the crackle of bonfires, you who are the golden Sun and glowing lava, Spirit of the Phoenix, Spirit of the Flame Dancers, hear me, bring into these rites, your spirit of creativity and passion. Blessings and welcome!

I call to the West and the Element of Water, you who are the Undines of the rivers, and the Sirens of the crashing ocean waves, you who are the Naiads of the Grottos, come to me. Spirit of the Shark, hear me, bring to these rites, your deepest intuition and truest emotions, teach me to be flexible, to adapt and flow, like your waters. Blessings and welcome!

I call to the North and the Element of Earth, you who are bone and crystal, you who are tree and root and branch, Spirit of the Wolf, Spirit of the Gnome, I call upon you. Bring to these rites your spirit of prosperity, of stability and manifestation. Blessings and welcome!

Invocation to Deity:

I call upon Diana, Goddess of the witches and the hunt, join this rite today and bring with you magic and protection. Blessings and welcome!

The Waning Moon phase is good for removing things, getting rid of obstacles, relieving illness and pain, banishing negative thoughts, releasing pain, guilt anger, anxiety and bad habits. It's time to let go of all that does not serve your higher good!

Place your dark candle in a suitable holder, put it on your altar and light it (don't light any other candles on your altar).

Take the dried, salted herb leaves and slowly burn each one in the flame of the candle (you might want to drop them into a cauldron or flame-proof dish as you do this, as the salt will make the flame spit). As each leaf burns say out loud what it is you wish to be rid of, burn the bad habits, bad cycles, unwanted energies and say goodbye to that which h no longer serves you for the greater good.

When you have burnt all the herbs, sit quietly in front of the candle and clear out the negative thoughts from your mind and replace them with positive ones. Fill the void that you have just made with happy images and new plans.

If possible, allow the candle to burn out (safely).

Thank the quarters, saying:

Guardians to the Element of Earth, I thank you for your presence in this rite, I bid you blessings and farewell.

Guardians to the Element of Water, I thank you for your presence in this rite, I bid you blessings and farewell.

Guardians to the Element of Fire, I thank you for your presence in this rite, I bid you blessings and farewell.

Guardians to the Element of Air, I thank you for your presence in this rite, I bid you blessings and farewell.

Thank Deity, saying:

Diana, goddess of the witches and the hunt, I thank you for your presence in this rite, may your magic and protection stay with me. Blessings and farewell.

Uncast the circle, walking widdershins. Say:

This circle is open but never broken.

Waning Moon Releasing Worry and Stress Spell
What you need:

White candle
Black candle
Pink candle

Light a white candle to symbolise peace. While watching the flame, meditate on the question, what does peace mean to you?

Next light a black candle, this will absorb negative energies. Visualise any worries or stresses that you have being taken from you and into the black candle, which will transform that energy into positive vibes.

Now take a piece of paper and write down something that you wish to release or transform, then light the corner of the paper on the candle flame and drop it into your cauldron (or flame proof dish). Allow it to burn out and, as it does so, let it too take your worries and stresses with it. You can repeat this part as many times as you feel you need to.

When you are ready, snuff out the black candle. Next light a pink candle and focus on filling that void with positive and happy thoughts, wishes and plans. When you banish negative energy, you MUST fill it with positive energy otherwise the negative pattern will be repeated.

When you are finished, snuff out the pink and white candles.

You can repeat this spell over the course of several days until you feel you are done. If there are any candle stubs left bury them in the earth.

Waning Moon Reversing Spell

On occasion, unfortunately we may feel like we have been hit with a curse, a run of bad luck or even perhaps someone sending negative energy our way. This spell will reverse it.

What you need:

A small mirror
A black candle
A small dish of water

You need to set the mirror so that you can sit comfortably in front of it and see the reflection of your face, and also the reflection of the candle. Keep the room dark if possible and light the candle. Visualise any negative energy that has been sent your way or bad luck that has beset you being reflected away from you. As you visualise this happening, slowly move backwards away from the mirror until you are out of focus and the only reflection that remains in the mirror is the candle flame. When you feel all the negative energy has been reflected away, put out the candle with the water. Bury the candle stub in the earth.

Waning Moon Spell to Banish Depression

Depression is quite frankly horrible and sometimes it can be an incredibly difficult frame of mind to get out of. Working this spell on the Waning Moon phase can help.

You will need:

A few black candles
Water (preferably spring water)
A glass jug

A handful of soil made into mud with a little tap water
A glass bowl
Rose petals

Light a black candle and fill the glass jug with water, leaving about an inch free at the top. Stand the jug in front of the candle and focus on the flame, see the flame as the light in the dark tunnel, the light represents your life before the depression cloud came into it. Now put the handful of mud into the jug of water. Watch as the mud makes the water cloudy, visualise that mud as your depression. See the mud and your depression being dissolved in the water, allowing yourself to be released from its hold.

Snuff the candle out but leave it and the jug where they are. Fill the glass bowl with water and sprinkle the rose petals on the surface. Wash your hands in the water. The next day, light another black candle and replace the first one. See the water clearing gradually. Keep lighting a new candle each day and visualising the water as your life, being freed from the grip of depression.

When you are ready throw the water away, as far away as you can (outside of course!) and let that water carry any remaining threads of depression away with it.

Dark Moon/Balsamic

This is the time after the Waning Moon has disappeared from view and before the New Moon is visible, when the sky is dark and there is nothing to see. The sky is literally 'completely dark'.

This phase is magically good for addictions, change, divorce, enemies, justice, obstacles, quarrels, removal, separation, stopping stalkers and theft.

It can also be associated with universal love of self and others. The Dark Moon energy draws love to you and removes sorrows and past hurts. Calming, protective and serene, it improves relationships. This is also a good time for divination.

When the last quarter of the Moon has disappeared, write the name of something you wish to decrease on to the side of a black candle, and burn it every night until the New Moon. (Be careful here, you might want to state 'and harm none'). Leave your altar bare of flowers at this time. Burn only dark coloured candles or none at all. Use sombre incense such as myrrh and patchouli. Raise energy with slow drumming or chanting, or keep your rites low key. Call on the wisdom of the crone goddesses. Use this time to eliminate or banish bad habits.

You may feel more like meditating and being alone. Clear spaces of all descriptions and make endings. Some people favour scrying and meditation with the Dark Moon because it is a more inward time. The insights you glean now will have a deeper more insightful quality, whereas at Full Moon they may be more obviously creative.

Dark Moon Colours
Black, dark purple, dark blue.

Dark Moon Crystals
Obsidian, apache tears, rainbow obsidian.

Dark Moon Herbs, Oils and Incense Ingredients

Myrrh, bay, frankincense, jasmine, rose, elder, damiana, angelica, sage, borage, cinnamon, marigold, mugwort, rowan, saffron, star anise, thyme, camphor, dandelion, pomegranate, patchouli and yarrow.

Dark Moon Oil Recipe

7 drops jasmine essential oil
3 drops patchouli essential oil
1 drop sandalwood essential oil
Add these to a base oil such as sweet almond or grape seed
(about 15mls of carrier oil should be about right).

Dark Moon Incense Recipe

1 part dried jasmine flowers
1 part myrrh resin
1 part dried rose petals
1/2 part dried elder leaves
A few drops of myrrh essential oil

Dark Moon Bath Salts

1 cup sea salt
8 drops magnolia essential oil
3 drops pine essential oil
4 drops geranium essential oil

Dark Moon Meditation

Relax and make yourself comfortable, close your eyes and focus on your breathing, deep breaths in and out... Visualise the real world disappearing.

As your world dissipates around you, find yourself at the entrance to a cave. Outside there is a fire burning with a large cauldron on a stand hanging above it.

You make your way to the fire and begin to take in the delicious aroma wafting from the pot.

Surrounding the fire are blankets and cushions. As you reach the fire you hear the sound of movements from within the cave. Then an old crone appears from the cave mouth carrying a bunch of dried herbs. She looks up and greets you with a nod and invites you to join her, gesturing for you to sit on the cushions surrounding the fire.

As you make yourself comfortable, she drops the dried herbs into the cauldron and gives it a stir, creating more of the delicious scent to fill the air. She then sits herself down next to you and stares into the flames of the fire. After a short while she turns to you and asks, 'What are you searching for, child?'

You ponder her question for a moment and then answer her…

She sits quietly for a few moments and then gives you her answer. You reply to her with any other queries you have, she responds with her thoughts.

When you have finished talking she reaches into her pocket, draws her hand back out and hands an item to you. Take it and thank her.

When you are ready stand up and thank the crone.

Make your way back to this reality, stamp your feet and wriggle your fingers. What did the crone gift you with and what meaning does it have for you?

Dark Moon Ritual

You will need:

A green candle
A cauldron or flame proof dish
Paper and pen

Cast the circle, saying:

Maiden cast this circle white
Free from shadow, pure and light
Mother cast this circle red
Cast any negativity from our head
Crone cast this circle black
Grant us the knowledge that we lack
This circle is now cast unbroken.

Calling the quarters, saying:

I call to the East and the Element of Air, you who are mist and cloud, you who are fresh breeze and wild hurricane, Spirit of the Hawk, Spirit of the Sylph, hear me, bring into these rites purification and clarity, sweep through and remove stagnation. Blessings and welcome!

I call to the South and the Element of Fire, you who are the crackle of bonfires, you who are the golden Sun and glowing lava, Spirit of the Phoenix, Spirit of the Flame Dancers, hear me, bring into these rites, your spirit of creativity and passion. Blessings and welcome!

I call to the West and the Element of Water, you who are the Undines of the rivers, and the Sirens of the crashing ocean waves, you who are the Naiads of the Grottos, come to me. Spirit of the Shark, hear me, bring into these rites, your deepest intuition and truest emotions, teach me to be flexible, to adapt and flow, like your waters. Blessings and welcome!

I call to the North and the Element of Earth, you who are bone and crystal, you who are tree and root and branch, Spirit of the Wolf, Spirit of the Gnome, I call upon you. Bring into these rites, your spirit of prosperity, of stability and manifestation. Blessings and welcome!

Invocation to Deity. Say:

I call upon Arianrhod, Dark Moon Goddess and Lady of the Silver wheel, join this rite today and bring with you powers of renewal and rebirth. Blessings and welcome!

Use the power of the Dark Moon to look within, take time to contemplate. You removed all those unwanted energies at the Waning Moon, now it is time to go inwards and see what your real desires are.

Light your green candle.

Take your paper and write your dreams and desires on them, as many as you wish with one goal per piece of paper. Stack them on top of each other and place them in front of you.

If you are using a wand or an athame (ceremonial knife), tap each piece of paper, one at a time. Visualise powerful white light coming from the end and pulsing through the paper (if you aren't using any tools just use your finger tip). Then light each paper from the green candle and drop it into the cauldron or dish. As you do so each time send a blessing to the Divine.

When you are finished, snuff the candle out. After the ritual, take the ashes from the paper and either cast them into flowing water or bury them in the earth.

You might also like to sit for a while and meditate. Ask Arianrhod to show you at least some of your past lives...

Thank the quarters. Say:

Guardians to the Element of Earth, I thank you for your presence in this rite, I bid you blessings and farewell.

Guardians to the Element of Water, I thank you for your presence in this rite, I bid you blessings and farewell.

Guardians to the Element of Fire, I thank you for your presence in this rite, I bid you blessings and farewell.

139

Guardians to the Element of Air, I thank you for your presence in this rite, I bid you blessings and farewell.

Thank Deity, saying:

Arianrhod, Dark Moon Goddess and Lady of the Silver Wheel, I thank you for your presence in this rite, may your powers of renewal stay with me. Blessings and farewell.

Uncast the circle, walking widdershins. Say:

This circle is open but never broken.

Dark Moon Dream Charm

The beautiful flowers of the jasmine are ruled by the Moon. They work especially well in a medicine pouch or incense blend on the Dark Moon to bring about deep and meaningful dreams.

Dark Moon Spell to Protect Your House

This one is seriously easy and will place your home in a protective shell.

The only item you need for this spell is your own power. Sit quietly in the centre of your home, relax and centre yourself. Get a visualisation of your house into your mind. Take in all the details then, drawing on energy from Mother Earth, see a ring of powerful white protective light come up from the Earth around the boundaries of your property. Watch as it grows upwards and forms a protective bubble around your home.

The protective shield is now in place around your house. Every so often when you have a moment just sit and strengthen the shield with your mind and the power of Mother Earth energy.

Dark Moon Spell to Move Forward

Life lessons can occasionally leave us floundering and wondering how to pick up the pieces and move on with life. This spell should help.

What you need:

A photograph of the person involved (such as your ex) or an image of the situation that caused your life to fall apart
A cauldron or fire-proof dish
A sprig of leaves or herbs of your choice
A small pouch or bag (I use the little wedding favour bags you can pick up easily from craft stores or a small pouch made from felt).

Set light to the corner of the photograph and drop it into the cauldron to burn. Watch the flame and visualise all the pain, hurt and anguish you have experienced being released from you. Keep visualising the smoke from the flame taking those negative energies away. When you are ready, take the sprig of herbs/leaves and hold them in your hands. Send whatever negative energies you have remaining into those herbs, then bring your hands up to your forehead and visualise happy and joyful images replacing the hurtful and negative ones.

End by putting the herbs and ashes of the photograph into the pouch or bag. Take it away from your house and bury it. (I also find that throwing it in the dustbin the day the bins are emptied works too, as the dustbin truck takes care of removing it for me!)

When you dispose of the pouch take a minute or two to remember the good times you had before trouble set in.

Blue Moon, Red Moon and Eclipses

Blue Moon

Every so often we get a second Full Moon in a month and sometimes we actually get four Full Moons in a single season. Such Full Moons are called Blue Moons or sometimes 'Goal Moons'. Sadly, the Moon doesn't actually change colour, it looks just the same as the usual Full Moon.

The term 'Blue Moon' seems to only be a few hundred years old. References in history to a Blue Moon were improbable events or things that would not normally happen. This evolved to mean a rare occurrence or happening, and has led to the saying 'once in a blue moon'.

There is a belief that the Blue Moon holds the knowledge of the Crone and, therefore, all the wisdom of the Triple Goddesses combined. It is also said that the Blue Moon brings a time of heightened communication and connection with the Divine and the spirit world.

I would work magic on a Blue Moon for something that seems unobtainable or difficult to achieve... go with the thought that whatever your intent is, the outcome might just happen 'once in a Blue Moon'.

A Blue Moon Magic Spell

You will need:

A square piece of blue fabric, felt works well. You can even decorate it with Moons if you like.
Safety pins
Paper and pen
Length of cord or ribbon, gold or silver would be good

Lay out your items and calm, ground and centre yourself.

Then make a list of all the things that you would like but you think are unobtainable, the sort of things that you think you could never achieve or own.

Once you have written your list go back over it and really think hard. Double check all of the things you wrote down. Are there some that you don't really, really want? Are there some that in reality wouldn't work for you? If there are cross them off.

Once you have narrowed down your list cut your paper into strips and write a wish on each piece. Be positive when you write each one down, and visualise it happening.

Then, using the safety pins, pin each piece of paper to the blue cloth. Once you have pinned them all fold the cloth up and tie it with the ribbon or cord.

When the Full Blue Moon is risen take the bundle outside and hold it up to her, then make your request that your wishes be fulfilled, but don't forget to thank the Goddess. You can write a poem or chant to say at this time if you wish.

Once you are done, put the bundle somewhere that you can see it regularly, on your altar would be a good place.

Then wait and see what happens...

Red Blood Moon

October's Full Moon is sometimes called the Hunter's Moon or the Blood Moon. The name comes from hunters who would track and kill their prey by the autumn moonlight, preparing their food stores for the winter.

The Red Blood Moon represents abundance, harvest and gathering, and is a time to honour the Gods and Goddesses that correspond to hunting to give thanks for the bountiful harvest and for providing for us. In magical terms this equates to workings for abundance in your life, whether it is financial or spiritual, for good health, friendships, relationships and love.

Eclipses

A lunar eclipse is a powerful time to work magic as the energies of the Moon are amplified and focused. This is a perfect time for making major transformations, releases and changes in your life.

Take some time to meditate and look at the areas of your life that need a new injection, fresh ideas and new perspectives. Also look at what blockages are keeping you from achieving your goals and dreams. Release any of the negative energy that is stopping you from following your path and focus on your new goals. Be a phoenix rising from the ashes.

If you work magic on a lunar eclipse, just remember that the power that comes with it can be a bit unpredictable. Know what you are doing and how to handle it!

Moon Diaries and Moon Time

Moon Diary

I would also encourage you to keep a Moon diary, as she is so powerful, she can affect our moods, thoughts and feelings. If you chart the Moon phases and how they affect you and your emotions, you will soon begin to see a pattern emerge.

On each New Moon and Full Moon light a candle on your altar and focus on the energies.

Honouring Your Moon Time

Sorry guys, this one is more for the ladies, but if you have a lady in your life, you might notice her moods change... ahem...

Society has taught us that periods are to be hated and sometimes, for some people, they can be quite physically unpleasant. However, I believe if we honour our monthly cycle we can learn to work with our bodies and hopefully lessen some of the more uncomfortable side effects that a period can bring. Having a period celebrates you being a woman; it echoes Mother Earth in the fact that a woman can create life in her own body. I have found personally, and in talking with others, that once you start following the phases of the Moon quite often your period will start to work in synch with her powers.

But the power of the Moon affecting our bodies, our emotions and our energy levels is not solely for women, it does affect men too. Although men don't have periods, the power of the Moon does play a part in moods and feelings – men can also track their moods to the Moon phases.

The Seasonal Moon

Witches celebrate eight seasonal festivals, the Sabbats, celebrating the cycles of nature and the process of growth, decay and rebirth that we are part of. Naturally, certain festivals lend themselves to being marked with a Full, Waxing or Waning Moon.

- Yule is a time of rebirth, when the Sun stops retreating, stands still (the meaning of the word solstice) and begins to return.
- Imbolc is when the first signs of spring growth are seen. Deep in the belly of the Earth life is stirring.
- Ostara is a festival of plant fertility and marks the time when day and night are equal in length.
- Beltane is a time when we celebrate human fertility, with the sacred marriage of the Earth Goddess and the Sun God.
- Litha is the climax of the seasonal cycle, when the hours of daylight are longest.
- Lughnasadgh is the first harvest, abundance is celebrated.
- Mabon, the last harvest, and the time when the mists are rising and the veil between the worlds is becoming thin.
- Samhain is when we mark the darkest time of the year, the death and decay that now must be gone through for new growth to arise.

The equinoxes and solstices are astronomical dates linked to the position of the Sun. The cross-quarter festivals are dependent upon the rhythms of plants and animals. It is not hard to see that different phases of the Moon may be linked to different festivals. In fact, the yearly cycle of the Sun is echoed by the monthly cycle of the Moon.

Yule for instance is associated with the New Moon and might be appropriately celebrated at this time, while Imbolc is associated with the first quarter, Beltane with pre-Full Moon, Litha with Full Moon and so into the waning cycle until Samhain at the approach of Dark Moon.

As you note the phases of the Moon and their effects, you may also tune into the different times of year. The wan, shrinking Moon haunting the small hours at Samhain may look all the more melancholy because of the late autumn, while a Full Moon around Beltane may seem even more luxuriant.

The Triple Goddess

The phases of the Moon can be associated with the Triple Moon Goddess and the aspects of womanhood; the Waxing Crescent Moon being the young Maiden, full of energy and potential, then the Full Moon is the Mother aspect, the nurturer and provider, followed by the Waning Crescent and Dark Moon as the Crone, the wise woman and keeper of mysteries. They represent the cycle of life – birth, death and rebirth.

The Maiden is enchanting, new beginnings, promise, youth, pure, excitement and carefree. She is the Goddess of beauty, love and hope. She has innocence about her. Her season is spring and her colour is white.

The Mother is fertility, stability, power, fulfilment and life. She is the Goddess of love, motherhood, protection, guidance, inner peace, intuition, psychic and spiritual development and care. Her season is summer and her colour is red.

The Crone is wisdom, compassion, knowing and is full of a lifetime of experience. She is the Goddess of wisdom and experience as well as death. Her season is winter and her colour is black. She is the last stage of life, but also a reminder that the cycle never ends, life is an ever-flowing cycle. Working with the Dark Goddess teaches us that we need death as a passage to another place; it is a part of our own lifecycle.

Triple Goddess Meditation

This meditation connects you with the Maiden, Mother and Crone aspects of your own personality. Gentlemen can do the same to connect with their feminine energies or they can replace the Maiden, Mother and Crone aspects with the male counterparts, the Youth, Warrior and Sage.

Make yourself comfortable, relax and focus on your breathing. Close your eyes. Take deep breaths in...and out... Visualise the real world disappearing.

As your world dissipates you find yourself in a swirling vortex of energy. Note what colour it is, feel the peace that the energy brings you, relax and allow it to carry you. As it carries you along allow it to take any negative energies, worries or stresses from you... the energy is taking you to your inner self...

Slowly the vortex of energy disappears and you find yourself in a beautiful place. What can you see? What are your surroundings? What can you hear and what scents can you detect?

The vortex has taken you to the realm of the Triple Goddess. It is day time but you can see a Crescent Moon waxing in the sky. The landscape around you is bright and alive. You feel content and peaceful.

As you look around you see a pool of water so you make your way over. The edges of the pool have been decorated with beautiful white flowers, and the water is so inviting you slip off your clothes and submerge yourself in the water. It makes you feel alive, refreshed and renewed, you feel young and energised. This is the energy of the Maiden, of the Waxing Moon.

As you make your way out of the water you find that someone has left you fresh towels so you dry and dress. Once you have done this you look up and see a Goddess approaching, she is young and beautiful...she is YOU in your maiden form. You sit with her for a while and talk... she may have advice for you; she may have answers or a gift for you...

The Maiden Goddess now departs so you wander over to the other side of the pool where you see a small altar covered with fruit and beautiful red flowers. In the centre of the altar is a mirror. You realise that while you have been talking to the Maiden, the Moon has become full in the sky.

You stand in front of the mirror and see yourself full of life, abundance and glowing. You watch yourself change from maiden to mother, embracing all that happens. You realise someone is coming towards you and turn to see a Mother Goddess. She is strong and beautiful.

She is you in your mother phase; she sits and talks with you and reminds you about the qualities of the mother within yourself, nurturing and caring but also reminds you not to neglect yourself and your own well-being. Talk with her, listen to her and accept any advice or gifts she gives you. She is the life force. When you are finished, she departs.

You realise that the Moon in the sky has now turned into a Waning Crescent. You look around and see a crossroads, at the side of it sits a Crone Goddess beside her cauldron so you make your way over to her. She asks you to sit with her. She is a crone, but still beautiful. She is you in your crone phase, the Dark Mother, the wise woman.

Sit and talk with her, ask her questions, listen to her advice. She will ask you to acknowledge yourself as your own source of wisdom and power. Leave behind any doubts or insecurities of the Maiden, the emotional aspects of the Mother and find the centre of yourself, the core, the part of you that connects with spirit. The Crone Goddess asks you to acknowledge the dark side of you.

When you are ready you get up and thank the Crone Goddess then make your way back past the altar and then past the pool.

As you do so you feel the vortex of swirling energy take hold of you again, this time it brings you back to your own reality. Stamp your feet and wriggle your fingers to bring yourself back fully.

Moon Names

Each monthly Moon also has its own name. If you notice, each Moon name usually relates to the weather, the region, the culture, the season or an animal – these names reflect what was happening at the time of year for the native people. Each monthly Moon will also have its own specific magical properties and correspondences.

January
Wolf Moon, Quiet Moon, Snow Moon, Cold Moon, Chaste Moon, Disting Moon and Moon of Little Winter.

Work magic for beginnings, protection, personal issues, aiming for goals, hidden agendas and reversing spells.

February
Ice Moon, Storm Moon, Horning Moon, Hunger Moon, Wild Moon, Red and Cleansing Moon, Quickening Moon, Solmonath and Big Winter Moon.

Work magic for purification, healing, growth, responsibility, forgiveness, love of yourself and new plans.

March
Storm Moon, Seed Moon, Moon of Winds, Plow Moon, Worm Mon, Herthmonath, Lentzinmanoth, Lenting Moon, Sap Moon, Crow Moon and Moon of the Snowblind.

Work magic for prosperity, exploration, new beginnings, balance, truth, honesty and clarity in a situation.

April
Growing Moon, Hare Moon, Seed or Planting Moon, Planters' Moon, Budding Trees Moon, Eastermonath, Ostarmanoth, Pink.

Work magic for creativity, balance, change, confidence, opportunities, emotions and productivity.

May
Hare Moon, Merry Moon, Dyad Moon, Flower Moon, Frogs Return Moon, Thrilmilcmonath, Sproutkale, Winnemanoth, Planting Moon and Moon When the Ponies Shed.
Work magic for creativity, intuition, faerie magic, tree and plant magic, psychic work and spirit connections.

June
Mead Moon, Moon of Horses, Lovers Moon, Strong Sun Moon, Honey Moon, Aerra Litha, Brachmanoth, Strawberry Moon, Rose Moon and Moon of Making Fat.
Work magic for protection, strength, decisions, responsibility, personal issues and inner power.

July
Hay Moon, Wort Moon, Moon of Claiming, Moon of Blood, Blessing Moon, Maedmonat, Hewimanoth, Fallow Moon, Buck Moon and Thunder Moon.
Work magic for relaxation, preparation, success, dreams, divination, new plans, reaching your goals and spiritual work.

August
Corn Moon, Barley Moon, Dispute Moon, Wedmonath, Harvest Moon and Moon When Cherries Turn Black.
Work magic for harvesting projects, reaping what you sow, appreciation, health, good friendships and abundance.

September
Harvest Moon, Wine Moon, Singing Moon, Sturgeon Moon, Haligmonath, Witumanoth and Moon When Deer Paw the Earth.

Work magic for balance, organisation, cleansing, mental and spiritual clearing out and finding peace.

October

Blood Moon, Harvest Moon, Hunter's Moon, Shedding Moon, Winterfelleth, Windermanoth, Falling Leaf Moon, Ten Colds Moon and Moon of the Changing Seasons.

Work magic for divination, spirit contact, death and rebirth, justice, balance, harmony and letting go of that which does not serve your higher good.

November

Snow Moon, Dark Moon, Fog Moon, Beaver Moon, Mourning Moon, Blotmanoth, Herbistmanoth, Mad Moon, Moon of Storms and Moon when deer shed antlers.

Work magic for transformation, preparation, strength, communication with the divine and inner work.

December

Cold Moon, Oak Moon, Wolf Moon, Moon of Long Nights, Long Nights Moon, Aerra Geola, Wintermonat, Heilagmanoth, Big Winter Moon and Moon of Popping Trees.

Work magic for death and rebirth, balance, spiritual matters, family, friendships, relationships, shadow work and personal issues.

Celtic Tree Calendar

I am not sure how old the Celtic Tree calendar is. Some say it is as ancient as the Ogham, some say it is a more modern invention by author Robert Graves. However, it is a lovely calendar to follow and is based on thirteen months, each named for trees, all based on the Ogham. My own coven uses the Full Moon of each of the tree months for our ritual celebrations.

Beth (Birch) December 24 to January 20
A time of rebirth and regeneration, new projects and new endeavours. It is a time to look towards the light again and a time of change.

Luis (Rowan) January 21 to February 17
This Moon is associated with the Goddess Brighid. It is a good time of year to perform initiations or self-dedications. It represents intuition, protection and inner vision.

Nion (Ash) February 18 to March 17
The Ash is the World Tree, Yggdrasil. This is a month for working inner magic and spiritual journeys. It is a good time to connect with the energies of all the worlds, seen and unseen.

Fearn (Alder) March 18 to April 14
Alder is a tree of balance and for action from inspiration. This is a good month for working divination and with prophecies as well as for boosting your own intuition.

Saille (Willow) April 15 to May 12
Willow is a tree of healing and protection. It can help us to connect with our emotions and bring us inner strength.

Uath (Hawthorn) May 13 to June 9

This Moon month is about fertility, male energy and fire. The hawthorn is good for protection and is said to grow by the entrances to the faerie world.

Duir (Oak) June 10 to July 7

Such a powerful and strong tree, Oak brings the magical energies of inner strength and courage. This is a good month for working strength and protection spells along with any prosperity ones too.

Tinne (Holly) July 8 to August 4

Holly is a tree of balance, luck and protection. The tree can help with restoring direction and bringing balance into your life as well as helping with emotional situations.

Coll (Hazel) August 5 to September 1

This is the Jedi tree. It carries with it the magical energies to help you tap into the life force that is within you. It is all about creativity and inspiration to bring about good changes.

Muin (Vine) September 2 to September 29

Grapes! Which means harvest, so this month is all about reaping what you have sown. This is a good month for re-gaining balance and bringing happiness and passion into your life.

Gort (Ivy) September 30 to October 27

Ivy reminds us of the circle of life, that death means rebirth. This is a good time of year to get rid of any negativity from your life; a time to make improvements.

Ngetal (Reed) October 28 to November 24

Yep, I know a reed isn't technically a tree! Reed is connected with the Underworld and those souls that have passed. The

Reed Moon is a good time for scrying and divination and working with spirit guides.

Ruis (Elder) November 25 to December 23

A time of endings and new beginnings, of death and rebirth. Elder is a kind of phoenix tree to enable you to rise from the ashes. It is a time of regeneration and brings with it wisdom and understanding.

Moon Deities

There are thousands and thousands of different deities all with different energies and personalities, some of them are specifically aligned with Moon magic. The list below shows a small selection of them but it is by no means comprehensive.

Alignak: An Inuit God of the Moon and the weather, he also controls the tides, earthquakes and eclipses.

Andraste: An ancient British Goddess said to have been worshipped by Queen Boadicea and connected to the Moon. She is a goddess of war, but in her light aspect she rules love and fertility. Her animals are the raven and the hare.

Anuket: Egyptian Goddess of the Crescent Moon, agriculture and the Nile. She also looks after the poor. Her symbols are shells, coins and fish.

Arianrhod: Welsh Goddess of the Dark Moon, the stars, the sea, reincarnation, prophecy, dreams and the future. Her name means silver disc or wheel. She is part of the triple goddess triad with Blodeuwedd and Cerridwen. She is able to shapeshift into an owl. She receives the souls of the dead and guides them on. She is also one of the five goddesses of Avalon (along with Blodeuwedd, Branwen, Cerridwen and Rhiannon.

Artemis: Greek Goddess of the hunt and associated with the Crescent Moon. Her twin brother, Apollo, is associated with the Sun, so she gradually became a Moon goddess as a balance. She also rules forests, woodlands and wild animals and defends the weak and the young. Her symbols are the bow and arrow, the deer and the bear.

Artimpaasa: Scythian Goddess of the Moon and the tides. She also rules love and family relations.

Athene: Greek goddess of weaving, which is often a trait associated with the Moon. Athene is also Goddess of Wisdom and one of the three Greek virgin goddesses. She protects and defends and is also a philosopher. Her symbols are the owl and the olive tree.

Auchimalgen: A South American Moon Goddess. She is the spirit of compassion. She looks after the human race, protecting them and keeping evil away.

Bendis: Thracian Moon Goddess often associated with Artemis and Hecate. She is Goddess of hunting, mysteries, orgies, athletes and the Moon.

Blodeuwedd: A Welsh Goddess with a connection to both the Moon and death and reincarnation (aspects of the Dark Moon). She is the maiden of the Triple Goddess triad (with Arianrhod and Cerridwen). She is the May Queen, Goddess of spring, flowers and initiations. She is also known for her betrayal and manipulation.

Cerridwen: Welsh Goddess associated with the Full Moon. She is also Goddess of wisdom, inspiration and intuition. Keeper of the sacred cauldron in which she brews the 'awen', she represents spiritual transformation and justice. She covers all three aspects of the Triple Goddess, but also forms the triad with Blodeuwedd and Arianrhod. She rules prophecy and magic, death and rebirth. Her animal is the white sow.

Ch'ang-O: Chinese Moon Goddess. Ch'ang-O and her husband were banished from the upper world to live as mortals. She wanted to return so drank an immortality potion meant for both of them, which sent her floating up to the Moon where she is now destined to spend eternity. Her symbols are incense, sweet food and the hare.

Coyolxauhqui: An Aztec Goddess whose name means 'golden bells'. She died in the womb, killed by her brother who cut off her head and threw it up to the sky, where she now remains... as the Moon. She is often depicted as a beautiful maiden wearing clothes decorated with lunar images and bells.

Cybele: A Roman Underworld Goddess who is associated with the Dark Moon. She is mother of the Gods, fertility and nature. She also protects from war and invasion.

Demeter: Goddess of the Full Moon, the harvest and agriculture. She is the Mother aspect of the Triple Goddess triad with Persephone and Hecate. Her symbol is a cornucopia. She always looks after those in need.

Diana: A Roman goddess of the hunt, woodlands, forests and the Moon and Queen of the Witches. She is very beautiful, controls magic and protects women. She looks after all animals, those in slavery and the poor.

Ereshkigal: A Sumerian Goddess who was called Queen of the Underworld and in her aspect as the Crone is Goddess of the Dark Moon. She not only represents the dark and that which is unseen, but also the shadow of our personalities.

Freyja: Although not called a Moon Goddess, many of her attributes connect her with both the Full and Dark Moons. She is Goddess of love and war and a beautiful Maiden Goddess. She represents love, family, sensuality, souls of the dead and poetry.

Gleti: A Moon Goddess from West Africa, she is the mother of the stars and the planets ruling love and light. Her husband is the Sun God.

Hecate: The oldest Greek form of the Triple Goddess. She is connected to childbirth and maidenhood so has all aspects of the Moon phases, but is often connected to the Dark Moon as she represents magic, ghosts and the spirit world. Her powers cover Heaven, Earth and the Underworld; she is protector of the spirit world and associated with crossroads.

Imatar: The Finnish-Ugrian Goddess of the Crescent Moon.

Inanna of Sumeria: Also known as Ishtar in Babylon, Goddess of love and war, Queen of Heaven and Earth and the Full Moon, she is seen as the stars. Inanna is also Goddess of seduction, sensuality, fertility, mating, wisdom and the magic of life and death. Her war Goddess side protects her followers. Her symbols are the eight-pointed star and the lion.

Ix Chel: A Mayan Moon Goddess and mother of the Mayan deities, she rules life and death. She covers all aspects of womanhood from maiden to crone and represents creativity, inspiration, weaving, artists and musicians.

Maat: Egyptian Goddess of justice, order, truth, balance, law and the Crescent Moon. She measures the soul with her feather of truth to decide whether it goes to the land of the dead or is destroyed.

Mama Quilla/Mama Killa, Quillamama: Incan Goddess of time and the Full Moon. She keeps time flowing and is keeper of the calendar. She also protects married women.

Marama: Maori Moon Goddess from New Zealand. She is a Goddess of light and resurrection, collecting the souls of the dead and making sure they travel onwards away from the living.

Manidroe: A Norse God, son of Mundilfore, he rode the chariot of the Moon.

Mawu: From West Africa, this Goddess rules the Moon and the night she brings with her wisdom and embodies motherhood. She has a twin consort, Liza, who is a Sun God. Her symbol is the cowrie shell.

Neith: Egyptian Goddess of women, marriage, war, hunting, weaving and the Crescent Moon.

Nephthys: Egyptian Goddess of the dead, darkness, the mysteries of death and the Dark Moon. A powerful goddess, she protects souls, has great magical power, is Queen of the Underworld and offers rebirth.

Pajau Yan: Vietnamese goddess of health, healing and the Moon. She gives good fortune to the living and helps the dead to the underworld, she resides within the Moon.

Pasiphae: A three-faced Moon Goddess from Crete, a powerful witch and oracle. She also rules the Sun.

Parvati: Indian Goddess of feminine energies, womanhood, patience, artists, dancers, poets and the Crescent Moon. She is the Maiden from the Triple Goddess triad which includes Durga and Kali Ma.

Selene: A Greek Goddess of Moon magic, sleep, dreams, prophecy. Her brother is Helios, a Greek Sun God.

Sina: A Polynesian Goddess who lives within the Moon and protects night travellers. She travelled to the Moon in her canoe and loved it so much that she stayed!

Thoth: An Egyptian Moon God, he also represents magic and wisdom.

Venus: Roman Goddess of love, sex, beauty and is associated with the Full Moon. She removes trouble and anguish and brings joy and happiness; she is also the Goddess of prostitutes.

Vesta: Roman Goddess of hearth, home, fire, domesticity, family and the Crescent Moon.

Yemaya: African Goddess of water, the sea, feminine energies, women, pregnancy, birth, healing and the Moon.

Meditation to Meet a Moon Deity

Relax and make yourself comfortable, close your eyes and focus on your breathing, deep breaths in … and out… Visualise the real world disappearing.

As your world dissipates you find yourself in a stone building, as you turn around and take in your surroundings you realise you are in a courtyard with stone pillars all around you and beneath your feet is a beautiful mosaic floor.

You turn your head upwards and realise that the stone building has no roof and you can see the dark, indigo blue night sky. It is full of twinkling stars and a beautiful Moon shines its light into the centre of the courtyard.

You notice at one end of the courtyard there is a stone seat covered in cushions so you head towards it and make yourself comfortable.

Once you are seated you can take in the details of your surroundings. The pillars around the courtyard are painted with many wonderful lunar symbols and signs.

You then hear movement and look to see a figure heading towards you from across the courtyard. As they come into focus, what do they look like? What are they wearing? They come right over and sit beside you.

This is your opportunity to ask them any questions that you wish to. Spend as much time as you need to in conversation.

When you are ready, the deity hugs you and departs, with your thanks.

Make your way back to the courtyard entrance and back to this reality, stamp your feet and wriggle your fingers.

Magic to Honour the Moon

Make a Moon Altar

You could set up an altar to honour the phases of the Moon and the dark mysteries of the night. It doesn't have to be large, just a small shelf or corner of a sideboard. Go with your instincts (as always!) on what items to put on your altar, but here are some suggestions to get you started:

Candles: Change the colour for each different phase of the Moon. (I would suggest white for waxing, red for full and black for waning to represent the three phases of the Triple Goddess.) Or you could use white or silver candles for the Moon and darker ones for the night such as deep red, forest green, purple or dark blue.

Herbs, crystals, shells, bowl of water: Use crystals that symbolise the Moon phases or the night. Night crystals might be apache tears, obsidian, angelite, celestite, smokey quartz, fluorite, quartz, jet, blue beryl, moonstone, selenite, pearl, opal, onyx, sodalite, dark agates, aquamarine and mother of pearl.

Moon Power Animals

Place pictures of animal spirits on your altar that correspond with the Moon or the night-time. These are generally nocturnal creatures but you may find you connect with others, go with what shows itself to you. Some Moon power animal suggestions are:

Bat: (That's an obvious one, isn't it?) Bat medicine includes avoiding obstacles, barriers, transformation, releasing bad habits and personality traits, learning from past lives, journeying, intuition, understanding dreams, illusion and communication.

Cat: Cat medicine includes curiosity (of course!), love, mystery, independence, healing, magic, mystery, seeing the unseen, dreams, protection, feminine energies, intuition, telepathy, self-acceptance, fertility and foresight.

Jaguar: Jaguar medicine includes reclaiming your power, aggression, power, lunar energies, multi-tasking, solitary, clairaudience, inner visions, intuition, guide, teacher, mentor and magic.

Black Panther: Black panther medicine includes pacing yourself, fast response, meeting deadlines, depth of vision, psychic sight, inner knowing, passion, sensuality, feminine powers, the dark mother, the Dark Moon, power of the night, death and rebirth, cunning, strength, boldness, beauty, astral travel and otherworld journeying.

Moth: Moth medicine includes working with shadow, transformation, metamorphosis, ability to find light in the dark, hearing the unspoken word, psychic abilities, healing, optimism, letting go of negative energies and moving forward.

Owl: Owl medicine includes silent and swift movement, keen sight, unmasking deceit, an excellent underworld guide, wisdom, magic, darkness, freedom, dreams, shapeshifting, clairvoyance, astral projection, messages, finding the hidden truth, secrets and omens.

Wolf: Wolf medicine includes teaching, individuality, shape shifting, group consciousness, loyalty, devotion, talent, ritual, attention to detail, security, guardians, spirituality, truth, family, Moon energies, emotions, trust and intuition.

Cow and Bull: The bull symbolises fertility while the cow is a symbol of motherhood and nourishment. The cow is a very lunar energy while the bull symbolises the Sun, although his horns are in the shape of the Crescent Moon. The bull is earth, possessions, the mundane, the union of male and female, production, sowing new seeds, stubbornness, insensitivity, asserting your feminine energies and insecurity. Defending your family, being content, being aware of your surroundings, being alert, being conscientious and strong are all cow and bull medicine.

Crow: Crow medicine includes change, movement, mystery, illusion, the hidden and sacred, interpretation, trickery, symbols, omens, dreams, shadow work, hidden opportunities, shapeshifting, clairvoyance, intuition, introspection, wisdom, integrity, being mindful, truth, standards, change, the past, the future, messages, magic, opportunities, deception, unseen forces, light and dark and spiritual strength.

Dog: Dog medicine includes loyalty, devotion, protection, friendship, companionship, faithfulness, team spirit, dedication, communication, strength, stamina, hunting, retrieving, guardians, law, order and the underworld.

Dragon: The types and breeds of dragon are numerous and a whole book could be written on them alone. However, as a general guide, dragon medicine includes power, transformation, infinity, wisdom, the supernatural, change and guidance.

Hare: (Definitely a Moon animal, think 'moongazy'.) Hare medicine includes transformation, hidden teachings, intuition, messages, quick thinking, protection, fertility, not worrying about the future and Moon gazing.

Raven: Raven medicine includes introspection, courage, self-knowledge, magic, healing, creation, rebirth, secrets, shape shifting, respect, shifting consciousness, will, intention, mysteries, changes, spiritual awakening, inner work, transformation and mysticism.

Snake: Snake medicine includes fertility, healing, death, the otherworld, sexuality, sensuality, magic, mystery, rebirth, reincarnation, immortality, spirit, guardianship, protection, change, creativity, psychic energy, wisdom, understanding and connection with spirit.

Meditation to Meet Your Night Totem/Guardian

Relax and make yourself comfortable. Close your eyes. Focus on your breathing, deep breaths in...and out... Visualise the real world disappearing.

As your world dissipates you find yourself in a field, it is dusk and you smell the scent of the night air.

As you turn around and take in your surroundings the scene takes your breath away. On the horizon ahead of you is the ancient sacred site of Stonehenge, the stones penetrating the sky line.

You make your way towards the stones...

As you reach the outer stones you reach up and place your hands on one of them. Feel the deep, powerful Earth energy...

When you are ready, head to the centre of the stone circle and sit yourself down on the ground. Ask for your night totem to make itself known to you...

Sit quietly and watch the land, the stones and the sky... see what animal comes to you...

When a creature appears, see if you can communicate with them (don't worry if you don't meet an animal this time, sometimes it can take several attempts).

When you are ready, thank your night guide and know that when you need to connect with its energies again, it will come to you.

Make your way back out of the stone circle and back across the field.

Slowly come back to this reality, stamp your feet and wriggle your fingers.

Drawing Down the Moon

Most witches will have heard of, or experienced the rite called Drawing Down the Moon (you can draw down the Sun too). This ritual supposedly dates back to the Dianic witches of Thessaly from ancient Greece. It is a powerful ritual and can lead to a very moving experience that can shed light on every aspect of your life and inner being. It can also open up your psychic abilities. This is my interpretation of the Drawing Down the Moon ritual, there are more structured and ceremonial versions that can be found on the internet if you prefer. It is the art of drawing upon the power of the Moon to send you into a trance and to channel the power of the Goddess. In some covens or traditions, the High Priestess will say the Charge of the Goddess (the original was attributed to Doreen Valiente); to invoke her, I am sharing here a version of the Charge of the Goddess written by Lesley Lightbody:

Diana, Istarte, Kali-Maa
Athena, Rhiannon, Ishtar
Names forgotten, names remembered
As the Old ways are now honoured
Mother Goddess come hear our call
As we rejoice in the Spirit of the All
Invoking your name three times three
As we have great need of thee
Gathered round the sacred pyre
Woods are burned upon the hour
Sacred woods your numbers nine
We honour those forgotten by time
The Divine Mother resides in us all
But only some will answer the call
Seekers of knowledge search without

Within the answers are found without a doubt
Protector of the Forest Glen
Protector of animals and of men
As old as time, as ancient as space
Cast your circle, make a Sacred place
Honour the Mother, honour the Moon
The circle of life, the natures boon
Call Her name, She'll answer the prayer
Maiden, Mother or Crone with matted hair
By many names the Mother has been known
Her legends increase, her stories roam
A thousand names Our Lady has it's true
A cosmic keeper of the green and blue
Blessed are we that know her name
Blessed are we that feel no shame
Blessed are we to hear Her call
And honour the Goddess as our all

This ritual really needs to be performed outside as you need to be able to see the Moon, the Full Moon is preferable. Even if the sky is full of clouds, the power of the Full Moon will still be available to you.

Cast a circle and call the quarters as you would do for any ritual. Then slowly start breathing in the light of the Moon, filling your entire body with its beams. Make sure you do a bit of grounding through your feet to stop yourself from floating away though!

The purpose is to go into trance to enable the Goddess to channel through you. This can be done by invocations to her, but I find that starting to slowly spin myself around, swirling and twirling whilst trying to keep an eye on the Moon works well.

When you come to a stop the Moon seems to rush down towards you. As the power of the Moon enters your body you may get images or hear messages, these may be for you, but if you are in a group the messages may be for other members of the ritual. Speak out loud everything you hear and see, whether it is words, symbols or images.

When the messages have stopped you can kneel on the ground and have a scrying bowl filled with water in front of you. Make sure the moonlight shines directly onto the water, you may then also get more images in the surface of the water. When you have finished and closed your ritual, make sure to ground properly.

You may want to write down all the messages as soon as you finish as they do have a tendency to escape from your memory quite quickly!

In a coven it is generally the High Priestess who draws down the Moon, but it can also work very well with several members at the same time.

Astrological Moon Signs

Everyone, even those people who aren't even remotely interested in astrology, will probably know their horoscope sign. Although referred to as a 'star sign' it is actually your Sun sign and as everyone was born under one... you are also born under a Moon sign.

We are familiar with the Zodiac and the cycle that the Sun makes through its signs, but the Moon (and all the planets) also travels through them. The Moon passes through each entire sign in just over two days. The Moon's passage through the Zodiac signs takes slightly less than 28 days. There are 13 of these cycles in a year. This means that the Full Moon appears in a different sign of the Zodiac each month. The Moon is always opposite the Sun when it is full, so if you know what sign the Sun is occupying, the Full Moon will be in the opposite sign of the Zodiac. (The Moon moves faster than the Sun).

If you can work your magic when the Moon is in a specific sign of the Zodiac it will add a lot of power to the working. If you add to that the correct Moon phase then you will have huge amounts of oomph!

Aries

General: Action, taking risks, independence. For bringing in energy and enthusiasm to your plans or new ventures. Expression, self-reliance, enthusiasm and spontaneity. Watch out for impulses, impatience, lack of energy and organisation and tempers.

- **New Moon:** Confidence, learning, fear and anger control, new projects and taking risks.

- **Full Moon:** Social situations, romance, music, honour.
- **Element:** Fire.
- **Colours:** Red.
- **Incense:** Cinnamon, basil, nettle, chervil, ginseng, pine, ginger, wormwood, geranium.
- **Aries Incense Blend:** Equal parts of cedar, ginseng, basil and pine with a few drops of ginger essential oil.

Taurus

General: Practical matters, permanence, sex, financial security, prosperity, confidence to speak out, growth of any kind, stability, peace, affection, devotion and harmony, staying power, bringing love into your life. Watch out for greed, stubbornness, possessiveness and wanting to have your own way!

- **New Moon:** Prosperity, harmony, investing, long term goals, love, healing and peace.
- **Full Moon:** Success, money, serenity and investments.
- **Element:** Earth.
- **Colours:** Pale to medium blue, green, pink, rose, mauve, burnt orange.
- **Incense:** Benzoin, mint, thyme, violet, marsh-mallow, mugwort, vervain, catnip
- **Taurus Incense Blend:** Equal parts of mugwort, vervain and thyme with a few drops of benzoin essential oil.

Gemini

General: Playing with ideas, learning, intellect, multi-tasking, communicating (although this is not good for permanent changes), short-distance travel, business communication, deals and transactions, sorting out disputes. Watch out for manipulation, lack of focus, disorganisation and back stabbing.

- **New Moon:** Learning, research, balance, meditation, divination, learning, family matters, clearing out the old and moving onto the new.
- **Full Moon:** Magic, messages, healing and religion.
- **Element:** Air.
- **Colours:** Blue, yellow, violet.
- **Incense:** Lavender, dill, parsley, anise, rosemary, sage, lemon grass, marjoram.
- **Gemini Incense Blend:** Equal parts of lemon grass, sage and lavender with a few drops of rosemary essential oil.

Cancer

General: Home, children and family (but watch for others' sensitivities), motherhood, pregnancy, finding a new home, exploration of past lives, scrying, divination, finding household decorations that you would like, emotions, psychic work, protection and sympathy. Watch out for mood swings, finding fault in others, irritability, judging others and dwelling on the negative.

- **New Moon:** Feminine matters, peace, protection, psychic skills, dreams, divination, drawing positive energy, pregnancy and emotions.
- **Full Moon:** Stability, home and family matters.
- **Element:** Water.
- **Colours:** white, silver.
- **Incense:** Damiana, sage, aloe, feverfew, heather, myrrh, chamomile, lemon balm, bay, parsley.
- **Cancer Incense Blend:** Equal parts of chamomile, feverfew, heather and myrrh with a few drops of myrrh essential oil.

Leo

General: Vitality, the heart, strong feelings, entertainment, opportunity, fertility, confidence, courage, strength, kindness, leadership abilities, bringing money to you (but only if it is badly needed). Watch out for selfishness, arrogance, stubbornness and bullying.

- **New Moon:** Courage, strength, positive thinking, success, loyalty, talents, having fun and generosity.
- **Full Moon:** Humanitarian issues, personal goals and groups.
- **Element:** Fire.
- **Colours:** Gold, deep yellow, bright orange.
- **Incense:** Frankincense, sunflower, lemon balm, chamomile, tarragon, cinnamon, orange, ginger, eyebright.
- **Leo Incense Blend:** Equal parts of dried orange peel, cinnamon stick and frankincense with a few drops of ginger oil.

Virgo

General: Organisation, detail, health, reaping your just rewards, fitness, refining your diet, purification, acquiring or improving skills, ensuring a good 'harvest' from a project, analysis, logical choices, precision and solutions. Watch out for criticism, arguments, control and lack of trust.

- **New Moon:** Problem solving, information, choices, accuracy, inner work and finding mistakes.
- **Full Moon:** Problem solving, intuition and divination.
- **Element:** Earth.
- **Colours:** Grey, green, black.
- **Incense:** Lemongrass, caraway, fennel, bergamot, dill, mint, horehound, marjoram.
- **Virgo Incense Blend:** Equal parts of fennel, mint and marjoram with a few drops of bergamot essential oil.

Libra

General: Contracts, partnership, love, beauty, cooperation, courtesy, charm, eloquence, friendships, bringing balance and harmony into your relationships, marriage, business contracts and agreements, legal matters, justice, increasing your social life, attracting love into your life. Watch out for judging others, unreliability, changeable attitude and a bit of chaos.

- **New Moon:** The arts, love, friendship, romance, cooperation, communication and partnerships.
- **Full Moon:** Social situations, decisions and justice.
- **Element:** Air.
- **Colours:** Pink, pale green, mauve, light blue.
- **Incense:** Rose, catnip, elderberry, thyme, St. John's Wort, lavender, mint, benzoin, bergamot.
- **Libra Incense Blend:** Equal parts of lavender, mint and thyme with a few drops of benzoin essential oil.

Scorpio

General: Loyalty, ownership (but watch out for suspicion and anger), matters requiring insight, increasing your libido or to attract passionate love (be careful though as relationships with a Scorpio influence are likely to be transformational and not always predictable!), healing of the mind and emotions, scrying, concentration, single mindedness, rebirth, transformation, wisdom, karma and instinct. Watch out for secrets, lies, jealousy, and suspicion, lack of forgiveness, grudges and hate.

- **New Moon:** Power, transformation, karma, instincts, clarity, wisdom, stop gossip, emotions, endings, death, rebirth and past life work.
- **Full Moon:** Energy, resources and transformation.
- **Element:** Water.
- **Colours:** Deep red.

- **Incense:** Basil, sage, catnip, coriander, sandalwood, thyme, nettle.
- **Scorpio Incense Blend:** Equal parts of sandalwood, thyme and sage with a few drops of coriander essential oil.

Sagittarius

General: Philosophy, adventure, journeys, study, honesty, imagination, long-distance travel, learning, writing and publishing, religion and philosophy, generosity, faith, understanding, hope and optimism. Watch out for no loyalty or commitment, emotional withdrawal, shifting blame and irresponsibility.

- **New Moon:** Projects, talents, understanding, hope, faith, awareness and travel.
- **Full Moon:** Knowledge and communication.
- **Element:** Fire.
- **Colours:** Purple, royal blue.
- **Incense:** Cedar wood, sage, basil, borage, saffron, nutmeg, sandalwood, chervil.
- **Sagittarius Incense Blend:** Equal parts of sage, nutmeg and cedar wood with a few drops of sandalwood essential oil.

Capricorn

General: Building, rules and regulations, discipline (this could be depressing), career matters, ambition, determination, spiritual matters, structure, self-discipline, sincerity and organisation. Watch out for pessimism, anxiety, feelings of failure and self-pity.

- **New Moon:** Authority, schools, savings, justice, promotion, order, self-discipline and sciences.

- **Full Moon:** Home, school and magical restructuring.
- **Element:** Earth.
- **Colours:** Black, dark green, dark blue, indigo.
- **Incense:** Myrrh, rosemary, tarragon, caraway, chamomile, mullein, patchouli, comfrey, Solomon's seal, marjoram.
- **Capricorn Incense Blend:** Equal parts of myrrh, rosemary and marjoram with a few drops of patchouli oil.

Aquarius

General: Inventions, social life, future goals, technology, science, forming and maintaining friendships, establishing groups, gaining more freedom or autonomy (be careful of bringing in rebellious energies though), developing intuition, independence, heightened perception and resourcefulness, becoming more detached or overcoming being too emotional. Watch out for unorganised thoughts, selfishness, not finishing projects and being opinionated.

- **New Moon:** Independence, change, love, new ideas, individuality and the sciences.
- **Full Moon:** Courage, loyalty, leadership, self-worth and independence.
- **Element:** Air.
- **Colours:** Electric blue.
- **Incense:** Eucalyptus, comfrey, rosemary, fennel, pine, clover, fenugreek, broom, violet, valerian.
- **Aquarius Incense Blend:** Equal parts pine, rosemary and fennel with a few drops of clover essential oil.

Pisces

General: Spiritual and psychic matters (but guard against confusion and deception), creativity, the arts, care, compassion, peace, devotion, inspiration and empathy, enhance or develop psychic abilities, letting life flow. Watch out for discontent, emotional imbalance, secrets, depression and lack of concentration.

- **New Moon:** Imagination, visualisation, dream work, divination, compassion, peace, seeing the big picture.
- **Full Moon:** Dream work, meditation and helping others.
- **Element:** Water.
- **Colours:** Sea green, sea blue, misty grey, pearly mauves and blues.
- **Incense:** Sage, basil, lemon balm, lemon, orris root, elder, borage.
- **Pisces Incense Blend:** Equal parts lemon balm, dried lemon peel and orris root with a few drops of lemon essential oil.

Moon Symbols

There are many symbols and signs associated with the Moon, the animal totem ones we have covered earlier, but we can add to that:

Boats: Egyptians used carved sky boats as symbols of the Moon and the Babylonians called the Moon the Boat of Light.

Circle: The Full Moon is often represented as a simple line drawing circle and, of course, her shape is that too. Some ancient stone circles may also have been built to represent the shape of the moon.

Crescent: The Waxing and Waning Moons are often depicted as a crescent shape (one either side of a circle to show the triple moon). Tip the crescent shape on its side and you also have the horns of the God and this shape can also be seen in a lot of ancient Moon deity headdresses.

Dew: Drops of dew are often associated with the Moon, washing your face in early morning dew after a Full Moon is said to bring you beauty.

Eye: The eye is very often used in Ancient Egyptian art as a representation of the Moon.

Fish: The fish is sometimes used as a symbol of the Moon, possibly connected to mermaids.

Frog: This creature is often associated with the Moon.

Grotto: A sacred space that contains a Moon tree where Moon deities were worshipped.

Horns: As previously mentioned, the crescent shape made by bull horns has connections with the Moon going back throughout history.

Horseshoe: Associated with luck but also the Moon due to its crescent shape.

Hounds: Dark hounds have often been connected with the dark energies of the Moon.

Mirror: Round-shaped mirrors are often representative of the Moon.

Pomegranate: With its red flesh and juice wrapped around the seeds, the pomegranate is not only a symbol of the dead but also of the Moon.

Sickle: Associated with the Moon due to its crescent shape again, but this time in the form of a sickle, which is often carried by druids.

Shell: I associate shells with water and emotions and that also links in with the energies of the Moon. I have a large round flat shell on my altar to symbolise the Full Moon.

Silver: Silver is a metal that has often been connected with the Moon. Maybe it is due to the colour, the alchemy or the magical properties or both.

Spiral: Think of the way a spiral works going up and down or in and out, this also echoes the phases of the Moon.

Well: Another connection between water and the Moon.

Willow Tree: A sacred Moon tree.

Wings: The Moon (and the Sun) are sometimes depicted with wings. I think this also has a connection to angels.

Yin and Yang: The Chinese symbol for balance and duality could also represent the light and the dark phases of the Moon.

The Moon at Home

You can bring the power of the Moon into your home by using ornaments and decorations. They don't have to be expensive, be creative!

Colours are a good place to start. The obvious ones are silver and, of course, white, but white and pale blue are good too along with pale greens and even lilacs. That could mean the colour of your walls, cushions, throws or candles. You could add in silver or crystal ornaments or bowls as well. The obvious ones are pictures and images of the Moon and the night sky as well as images of the Goddess.

White flowers work well too, along with incense and oils that have scents that correspond to the Moon phases.

Any water ideas can bring lunar energy into your home, such as a fish tank or one of the little indoor fountains that you can get or even shells to represent water.

Have fun with it!

Planting with the Moon

A lot of gardeners, even those who aren't witches, plant and harvest by the phases of the Moon. You can still find old almanacs that list what to plant and when in line with astrological timings. Think how much the Moon affects the sea and her tides, so it must affect the earth and how things grow too.

A Waxing Moon is good for planting. Fruit ready for eating straight away should be picked on a Waxing Moon; a Waning Moon is good for planting plants that fruit below ground such as potatoes. A Waning Moon is also good for pruning, weeding and harvesting food to be stored.

Just after a New Moon plant leafy vegetables and herb seeds. Waxing Moon gardening activities include potting cuttings, re-potting house plants and picking herbs, fruit and vegetables for eating straight away.

On a Full Moon plant vegetables such as tomatoes, peppers and onions (any type of 'watery' vegetables and fruit). Fertilise your plants on a Full Moon too.

Just after Full Moon plant tuber vegetables such as carrots and potatoes, also biennials and perennials.

On a waning Moon start a compost heap, weed, cut and prune, pick fruits and flowers, herbs and vegetables that will be stored.

Close to the Dark Moon cut timber and spray any fruit trees (preferably with eco-friendly spray).

Then you have the categories for the astrological signs; a list of each type of energy is show below, either barren, productive, semi-fruitful or fruitful:

Moon in Aries: Barren
Moon in Taurus: Productive
Moon in Gemini: Barren

Moon in Cancer: Fruitful
Moon in Leo: Barren
Moon in Virgo: Barren
Moon in Libra: Semi fruitful
Moon in Scorpio: Fruitful
Moon in Sagittarius: Barren
Moon in Capricorn: Productive
Moon in Aquarius: Barren
Moon in Pisces: Fruitful

Another useful guide is:

Above Soil-Level Plants: These are the plants that will produce crops above the ground; these should be sown the day after the New Moon up until the first quarter, preferably in a fertile or semi-fertile astrological sign.

Annuals: Plant the day after the New Moon up until the day before the first quarter, preferably in a fertile or semi-fertile astrological sign.

Below Soil-Level Plants: These are the plants that crop under the ground. These should be planted during the day after the Full Moon, preferably in a fertile or semi-fertile astrological sign.

Biennials and Perennials: This category includes shrubs and trees. Begin planting the day after the Full Moon and up to the day before the last quarter preferably in a fertile or semi-fertile astrological sign.

Seed Collection: This is best done at the Full Moon when the Moon is in a fire or air astrological sign such as Aries, Leo, Sagittarius, Libra, Gemini or Aquarius.

Harvesting: Picking fresh flowers and smaller harvests for magical use straight away, can be done in the early evening. If you want to dry and store the flowers and herbs, cut them mid-morning, after the dew has evaporated. Fruit and vegetables are best harvested during the Waning Moon and when the Moon is in a barren or semi-barren fire or air sign such as Aries, Leo, Sagittarius, Libra, Gemini or Aquarius.

Moon Cords

One way of 'collecting' and keeping Moon energy is by making a Moon cord. The cord is made on a particular phase of the Moon and the energy is trapped in each knot and kept there until needed. So, no matter what Moon phase it is, you always have the corresponding Moon energy to work your spell. Of course, it is easier and better to do any working on the actual Moon phase, but sometimes it just isn't possible, so if you have Moon cords to hand you don't have to wait.

To make a Moon cord, use wool, string, cord or thread about two feet long. It helps if you have different colours then you can use a different colour for each phase of the Moon, to help identify them afterwards. You will need to be able to see and feel the Moon to make your cord. Here, the choice is yours – you can cast a full circle if you wish, otherwise I like to just light a candle and invoke a suitable lunar deity then ask them to lend their power. Face the Moon and hold your cord up towards it. You can say prepared words then, or just ask for what you need – the power of that particular phase of the Moon to be drawn down into your cord for safekeeping until you need it.

You can also use the following:

By knot of ONE, the spell's begun
By knot of TWO, it cometh true
By knot of THREE, so mote it be
By knot of FOUR, this power I store
By knot of FIVE, the spell's alive
By knot of SIX, this spell I fix
By knot of SEVEN, events I'll leaven
By knot of EIGHT, it will be Fate
By knot of NINE, what's done is mine

As you visualise the power entering your cord, start tying knots – you will need to tie nine in total, each an equal distance apart. If you don't use the chant above, on your last knot it is an idea to finish with 'so mote it be'.

Thank the deity and the Moon for their energies.

Keep the cord safe. When you need the energy from that particular Moon phase place it on your altar, around your candle or wherever you are working your spell.

There are two modes of thought on using the cord, you can either keep using it and just recharge it at the next Moon phase or you can actually undo one of the knots each time you need that energy to 'release' it, once you have used all the knots you can recharge it.

Moon Charms

You can make all sorts of charms to honour or work with lunar energies, including small bottles or medicine bags filled with herbs, crystals and oils that correspond to the Moon. Even a small shell or plain crystal to carry in your pocket if charged with the energy of the Moon works well.

Herbs and oils associated with the Moon:

Aloe: Protection and luck
Lemon balm: Love, success and healing
Bladder wrack: Protection, the sea, the wind, money, psychic powers
Cabbage: Luck
Camellia: Money and prosperity
Camphor: Health and divination
Chickweed: Fidelity and love
Clary sage: Protection, love and visions
Coconut: Protection and purification
Cotton: Luck, healing and protection
Cucumber: Healing and fertility
Eucalyptus: Healing and protection
Gardenia: Love, peace, healing and spirituality
Grape: Fertility, mental powers and money
Honeysuckle: Money, psychic powers and protection
Honesty: Money and protection
Jasmine: Love, money and dreams
Lemon: Purification, love and friendship
Lettuce: Protection, love, divination and sleep
Lily: Protection
Lotus: Protection
Mallow: Love, protection and exorcism

Melon: Healing, purification, love and changes
Moonwort: Money and love
Moss: Luck and money
Myrrh: Protection, exorcism, healing and spirituality
Passion flower: Peace, sleep and friendship
Peach: Love, exorcism, fertility and wishes
Poppy: Fertility, love, sleep, money and luck
Potato: Healing
Sandalwood: Protection, wishes, healing, exorcism and spirituality
Willow: Love, protection and healing

Crystals associated with the Moon:

Amethyst: Love, integrity, stress relief, healing, addictions, patience, peaceful sleep, psychic protection, psychic powers and restoring energy.
Angelite: Secrets, truth, compassion, peace, tranquillity, angel communication and heightened awareness.
Aquamarine: Travel, healing, cleansing, communication, intuition, psychic awareness, meditation and clairvoyance.
Azurite: Dreams, guidance, inner wisdom, psychic powers, healing, communication, visions and spiritual connections.
Beryl: Protection, sympathy, happiness and sincerity.
Blue calcite: Protection, negotiations, confidence, scrying, wishes and meditation.
Blue chalcedony: Rebirth, good fortune, protection, practicality, learning, stress, psychic communication and protection from psychic attack.
Blue lace agate: Motherhood, stress relief, energy, peace, clairaudience and divination.
Celestite: Meditation, balance, attunement, clarity, writing, communication, spiritual work, dreaming, harmony and hope.

Jade: Healing, good fortune, prosperity, friendship, repels negativity and dream work.

Lapis lazuli: Calming, contentment, loyalty, integrity, trust, night magic, psychic protection and dream work.

Lepidolite: Peaceful sleep, pain relief, messages, support, cleansing, psychic work, negativity.

Moonstone: Stone of the Moon Goddesses, healing, intuition, dreams, tension, peaceful sleep, protection for travellers, psychic abilities, divination and prophecy.

Mother of Pearl: Secrets, pregnancy, motherhood, prosperity, sea magic and wishes.

Opal: Transformation, self-worth, confidence, self-esteem, creativity, justice, protection, harmony, seduction, emotions and karma.

Pearl: Harmony, women's mysteries, spiritual love and romance.

Quartz: Health, wealth, happiness, optimism, all sorts of healing, cleansing, energising, harmony, absorbing negative energy and psychic powers.

Sapphire: Spiritual healing, channelling, loyalty, commitment, psychic powers, clairvoyance, clairaudience and prophecy.

Selenite: Named after the Moon Goddess Selene, enchantment, ritual, fertility, motherhood, partnerships, communication, dispelling fear and psychic communication.

Moon Crystal Amulet

You can use any crystal or tumble stone that you like for this, go with your intuition and pick one that resonates with you and makes you feel a connection to the Moon.

If possible, do this outside under the Moon or in a window where the moonlight shines in. Sprinkle your chosen crystal with salt and then waft it through incense smoke to cleanse and purify it. After that very carefully pass the crystal over a candle flame and finally sprinkle it with Full Moon water.

Charge the crystal with your intent; it might be for protection, strength or courage, using the power of the moonlight.

Carry it with you in a small pouch, pocket or purse.

Moon Divination

The Full Moon, especially, is an excellent time to work with divination, as is the Dark Moon. The power of the Moon heightens your psychic senses. The Full Moon allows your creative and imaginative consciousness to surface, and the Dark Moon is a good time to reflect on your inner self.

I have mentioned a few ideas already within this book, but divination can be as simple as a bowl with a dark inside filled with water and set out so the moonlight shines into the water. You can also drop a silver coin into the bottom of the bowl to add to your reading, or sprinkle some herbs or drops of ink on the surface of the water to help create images.

Scrying is the art of seeing images or pictures in a surface, such as a bowl of water, a pond, a dark mirror or a crystal ball. Objects such as these are called speculums (which is Latin for the word mirror and not to be confused with the medical instrument of the same name!). The Elizabethan mathematician, astrologer and magician, John Dee, used many scrying devices including what he referred to as 'shew stones' – polished translucent or reflective objects, often made of obsidian that he used for his research.

Real crystal balls are incredibly expensive but I have had good results with smaller, cheaper glass globes. Set yourself up in a quiet place, I like to light a candle too. Ground and centre yourself and then gaze into the crystal, allowing your eyes to unfocus a little helps. Just let the images and shapes come to you.

A dark mirror is also an interesting speculum to use; these can be easily made by using a picture frame or old mirror and painting the back of the glass with black paint. Scry with your dark mirror in the same way you would a crystal ball.

Make sure you are relaxed and in a calm frame of mind, let yourself drift... Don't worry if you don't see much when you first try it, come away and try again later. Once you get the hang of it you will be able to ask specific questions. It helps to have a notebook handy to jot down any images or shapes you see; they might not make sense at the time but may do so later.

Dowsing is another form of divination that works well at the Full Moon. We normally associate the term dowsing with two hazel sticks used to find water or ley lines, but pendulums also fall under this category. There are many beautiful pendulums for sale in shops and on the internet, but they are also very easy to make. All you need is a piece of cord, string or chain and something fairly small but weighty to hang on the end of it – could be a stone with a hole in it, a shell, a small piece of wood or even a wedding ring!

You will also find that you don't always 'connect' with every type of pendulum, some will work with you, some won't, you will need to try them out to see. When you get or make a new pendulum it also helps to carry it with you for a while, and/or sleep with it under your pillow, just so that it attunes to your energies. It also helps to cleanse and charge your pendulum regularly by leaving it out in the moonlight, outside if you can do so safely, otherwise on a windowsill indoors is fine.

Start working with your pendulum by asking it simple questions such as 'give me a yes' and 'give me a no' so that you know which way it will swing to give you answers. Test it with questions so that you know how it works and how it will respond to you. Remember to keep your questions straightforward and simple, don't confuse it!

I find it also helps to thank my pendulum once it has given me an answer; it stops it from swinging so that I can move onto the next question.

Faeries, Angels and Werewolves

Moon Faeries

How you see, hear and experience faeries is a very personal thing, but for me a Moon Faery is a very ethereal looking nature spirit. She, and I say she, as I have only ever met female Moon Faeries, is pale and beautiful, almost transparent sometimes. They are only ever seen at night and are extremely elusive. I do feel that seeing or meeting a Moon Faery brings good fortune your way.

Be careful though, as with all faeries they have a dark side and a Moon Faery can capture your gaze and hold it and you could become trapped within her gaze...

Moon Angels

There are lots of angelic beings associated with the Moon, in fact there are as many angels as there are days of the month nearly... Angels associated with the moon include: Geniel, Enediel, Anixiel, Azariel, Gabriel, Dirachiel, Scheliel, Amnediel, Barbiel, Ardifiel, Neciel, Abdizuel, Jazeriel, Ergediel, Atliel, Azeruel, Adriel, Egibiel, Amutiel, Kyriel, Bethnael, Geliel, Requiel, Abrinael, Aziel, Tagriel, Atheniel and Amnixiel.

Werewolves

I had to put a piece in here about werewolves as they are always linked with the Moon. The official word for someone who turns into a wolf at the Full Moon is a lycanthrope. Back in medieval times if you were suspected of being a werewolf you were burnt to death. The legends suggest that the ways to become a lycanthrope are to be born a werewolf because of a curse that was placed upon you or your mother while she carried you, being a magician who could change willingly, or being bitten by another werewolf. There are also the legends that tell of Goddesses and Gods that could shapeshift into wolves.

Hollywood, of course, has taken this legend and made a huge fortune out of it. It is a shame really that the wolf comes out of this legend in such a bad light, because in reality the wolf is a very intelligent and social animal!

I think the connection with the werewolf legend is possibly one of transformation within, the Full Moon power being as strong as it is being the prompt for such a transition, the werewolf being the naked, raw animal part of our psyche... or perhaps werewolves really do exist...

Moon Crafts

Making a Moon Candle

If you are very crafty making your own candles is fun, but messy! Craft shops do sell pretty good candle making kits as well. However, you can always buy a readymade candle and decorate it yourself.

For a Moon Candle I would go with white to represent the Moon or you could tailor the colour to the Moon phase of white for waxing, red for full or black for waning, it is your choice.

Pillar candles are ideal for decorating as it gives you a bit more space to work. You can paint lunar images on the outside, stick crescent Moon shapes on it, tie ribbons around it, dress it with an oil Moon blend and roll it in crushed herbs or inscribe Moon symbols into the wax – be creative!

Moon Hanger

You can purchase wire circles in craft shops or if you are very patient and strong you can cut up a wire coat hanger and bend it into a circle shape. Cover your circle with ribbon by winding it around. Then tie three lengths of silver ribbon or cord equally around the circle so that they hang down. Then add whatever symbols, beads or bits and bobs you want to. Shells would be good as they have a connection to the Moon, sparkly crystals or small mirror pieces work well or cut out images from silver card, maybe in the shapes of your Moon animal totem or stick with crescent Moon shapes.

The Moon Tarot Card

One of the major arcana tarot cards is The Moon; you can use this card on your Moon altar or within spell workings, although you may have your own meanings for the Moon card, here are some of my thoughts on what it means:

- Illusion, underworld, emotions
- Something is blocking your light
- Pass through the gateway for the answers
- Veils of illusion, mysterious
- Struggle with the conscious
- Temptations, be careful
- Thresholds
- Superstition
- Deal with the areas of your life that need attention to find clarity and answers
- Threshold of a new experience or period in life
- Sometimes we have to look at the darker aspects of our personality to understand and move forward
- Listen and look for guidance
- You may have to deal with some uncomfortable home truths, it may not be what you want to see but it is necessary
- Are you ignoring or refusing to see something?
- This card totally says illusion and mystery to me, and dealing with the shadow self.

Moon Tarot Card Spell – Knowledge
This spell is to tap into your subconscious for knowledge.

You will need:

Three tarot cards – The Moon, The High Priestess and The Hermit.

Lay out the cards in order from left to right. Firstly, sit quietly and look at The Moon card, study it in detail, really seeing all the images, and think about its connection to your subconscious, your imagination, inspiration, dreams and intuition. Then move onto The High Priestess, think of your desire to seek knowledge and wisdom, perhaps to have insight into a mystery. Lastly look at The Hermit card, see the image as yourself holding a lantern up high to shine light onto the unknown, to illuminate the knowledge that you seek.

When you have finished with the visualisation, light a candle (blue or purple would work well but go with a colour that you are drawn to). Watch the flame of the candle and ask the Divine to grant you access to the hidden knowledge that you want to find. Sit for as long as you can watching the candle flame and meditating on the three tarot cards. When you are ready, snuff the candle. Watch out for signs and symbols as you go about your day, or if performing this spell in the evening take note of your dreams.

Moon Tarot Card Spell – Guilt

This spell uses The Moon tarot card to get rid of negative emotions and old guilt that tends to hang around making a nuisance of itself.

You will need:

Three tarot cards, the Moon, Judgement and The World
A white candle
A piece of paper and a pen
A cauldron or fire-proof dish

Make yourself comfortable and make sure you have all the items to hand.

Light the white candle then, sitting in front of the candle as it burns, write down on the piece of paper all the emotions and issues that have been causing you unrest, all the old guilt issues and negative thoughts. Take as much time as you need.

Then lay The Moon card down. As you do so think about all the words that you have written down, think how much pain they cause you and how heavy they make your energy. Come to the realisation that you must let go of these energies, you cannot change what happened in the past, and the negative energies you have created serve you no good.

As you feel the need to release these negative energies, screw the piece of paper with your list up in your hand then catch it on fire in the candle flame, dropping it into the cauldron and allowing it to burn.

As you watch the paper burning, lay down The Judgement card. See this card as your transformation, your rebirth. Call upon the power of the candle flame to purify you. The power of fire can cleanse, release and restore.

Then lay The World card down. This card represents you taking back your own power, replacing the negative energy with positive. You are refreshed, renewed and transformed.

When you are ready, snuff the candle out and bury any leftover stub along with the ashes of the paper in the earth.

And Finally...

She is so powerful and so wonderful – once you start working with the Moon and her phases a whole new way of thinking and working magic will open up to you...

Bibliography

Cunningham's Encyclopaedia of Magical Herbs by Scott Cunningham

A Complete Guide to Night Magic by Cassandra Eason

Healing Crystals by Cassandra Eason

Advanced Witchcraft by Edain McCoy

Solitary Witch by Silver Raven Wolf

Power of the Moon by Teresa Moorey

Moon Magic by DJ Conway

Tarot Spells by Janina Renee

MOON BOOKS
PAGANISM & SHAMANISM

What is Paganism? A religion, a spirituality, an alternative belief system, nature worship? You can find support for all these definitions (and many more) in dictionaries, encyclopaedias, and text books of religion, but subscribe to any one and the truth will evade you. Above all Paganism is a creative pursuit, an encounter with reality, an exploration of meaning and an expression of the soul. Druids, Heathens, Wiccans and others, all contribute their insights and literary riches to the Pagan tradition. Moon Books invites you to begin or to deepen your own encounter, right here, right now.

If you have enjoyed this book, why not tell other readers by posting a review on your preferred book site.

Readers of ebooks can buy or view any of these bestsellers by clicking on the live link in the title. Most titles are published in paperback and as an ebook. Paperbacks are available in traditional bookshops. Both print and ebook formats are available online.

Find more titles and sign up to our readers' newsletter http://www.johnhuntpublishing.com/paganism

For video content, author interviews and more, please subscribe to our YouTube channel.

MoonBooksPublishing

Follow us on social media for book news, promotions and more:

Facebook: Moon Books

Instagram: @MoonBooksCI

X: @MoonBooksCI

TikTok: @MoonBooksCI